Collecting Original Art

COLLECTING

JEFFREY H. LORIA

Foreword by Vincent Price

HARPER & ROW, PUBLISHERS

New York and London

ORIGINAL ART

Honoré Daumier, lithograph.

Dedication

FOR MY MOTHER AND FATHER AND FOR SUSAN

Contents

Illustrations

Foreword

Several years ago Sears, Roebuck and Co. asked me to put together a collection of original works of art to be shown and sold in their many stores. I was enormously excited, since it had always been my conviction that the merchandising of art to the American public at large had over the years become too restricted to a few large cities and too precious in its approach.

When it became apparent that I would need help in this vast project, I needed, ideally, someone young and art-adventurous with, preferably, a background in art history. I felt there would be little chance of finding anyone from the art departments of our universities, for these, while vital and productive, have up to now shown a tendency to turn their students inward toward scholarship and teaching, rather than giving them incentive or training to bring art out into the open where the so-called uninitiated could see and buy it. But when the project was announced by the press, I received a most welcome letter from, of all places, my old alma mater, Yale. Jeffrey Loria announced that he was graduating that spring, had majored in art, and was interested not only in getting art to people, but in selling it to them. So, with Sears' permission, I hired him.

Mr. Loria proved exceedingly excited with the whole concept. He was art knowledgeable (Yale had seen to that) but he was also art- and people-excited, and excitement is what is needed to put over any art project. Art is excitement which if we can't create ourselves, we can at least, through love of it, make available to others. This was the point, and Mr. Loria got it.

And, during the past few years, he has kept it and increased it and shared it with a vast public. He has found art, bought art, hung art, and sold art. Now in this book he explains art in the terms of "What is an original?" He discusses the thousand and one ways a work of art can be acquired, why artists are always the most curious of people, the most experimental. The book is excellent reading and will teach anyone the meaning of a very important word in the enjoyment of art—original.

I doubt if any serious collector, or even museum for that matter, hasn't been questioned or questioned themselves sometime or other about the origin-ality of some work of art. I know if in my beginnings as a collector I'd read this book, I might have avoided some sad mistakes. I had to learn the hard way. You can learn much more easily by reading this book.

VINCENT PRICE

Beverly Hills, 1965

Author's Note

I am grateful for the cooperation I have received from many sources. My primary thanks go to my wife Susan for her patience and encouragement and for the many long hours she willingly spent to help me edit this book.

To my friends at Sears goes a special vote of thanks for having made available to me material and information from the Vincent Price Collection which I have used in various parts of this book. In this connection, I am particularly appreciative of the cooperation of Messrs. George Struthers, Vincent Price, Harry G. Sundheim, and C. I. Pearson.

I must also acknowledge my many gallery and artist friends who have also contributed much valuable information and material which has helped make this book a reality. Last, I would like to thank my very good friend Eugene Santomasso of the Parsons School of Design for his critical advice and our long exchanges of views on art history.

Collecting Original Art

1 Taste, Knowledge, and the Collector

Honoré Daumier, lithograph.

The first steps of art collecting can be defined as a series of unique and personal experiences. Everyone has his own reasons for thinking that a certain work of art would be more desirable, pleasurable, and satisfying to own than another. Whether the collector makes this selection spontaneously, or partly on the basis of some knowledge of art history, art technique, market values, and cur-

rent vogues, his every choice is still an individual one, and his
over-all collection gives further testimony to this fact. It is distinct; it is self-expressive. Just as a work of art communicates the
thoughts and feelings of an artist, so an art collection speaks of
what the collector deems beautiful, meaningful, or technically
proficient. His possessions should reflect his personality and
uniqueness in the same way that an artist's creations express his,
for both collector and artist, whether consciously or not, are ex-
ternalizing and describing that intangible yet self-defining faculty
known as *taste*.

No one buys taste; some people have it instinctively, but many
people acquire it—not only by reading and by educating themselves, but also by training their eyes and their sensitivities. Taste
—one of the most important assets of the art collector—can be
developed gradually by observing your own collection and other
works of art you may encounter. Certainly the most significant
function of taste is to amplify your enjoyment and delight in
visual perceptions and experiences.

Pictures that come to say and mean more and more over a
period of time do so not only because they are innately excellent
but also because the viewer, at different stages of his own development, has learned new ways to analyze, define, and appreciate
them.

It is unjust to accuse anyone of "bad" taste in art once he has
made an effort to educate himself; no matter what the appearance
of his preferences, you must accept them as at least discriminating. Classify taste not as good or bad, but as educated or unedu-
cated, mature or immature.

Assuming, then, that taste is a matter of personal intelligence
and sensitive awareness, we cannot think that any work of fine art
is right or wrong to buy. People must buy what they like. Education and sensitivity are too widely diversified for us ever to expect
two people to have the same reactions to the same work of art. As
a matter of fact, it is more in keeping with the contemporary spirit

to recognize conflicting ideas, preferences, and tastes. What the artist was trying to say and whether or not he succeeded in saying it are matters for every viewer to decide for himself according to his own understanding of an artist's goals, materials, limitations, and talents. Anyone who sees and feels a given work as an accomplished statement should feel free to buy that work, regardless of trends or popular taste.

Art collecting means acquiring knowledge, both from formal learning and from mere observation. It means adjusting and attuning visual reactions and perceptions according to changing levels of experience and sophistication. When you know, for instance, how to differentiate and identify the various media of the original—a basic prerequisite for the purchase of fine art—you will react more critically to the shortcomings or strengths of particular oils as oils, watercolors as watercolors, engravings as engravings. You should also be able to instinctively recognize the fine distinctions between an etching and an aquatint, a black and white lithograph and a charcoal drawing, and other media sometimes confused with similar yet decidedly different counterparts. Most of all, your familiarity with all of the qualities of original techniques should enable you to decide confidently whether the works of art you see are original creations or photographic reproductions.

Having mastered the ability to differentiate the many media of fine art, you should proceed to study the "why" and "how" of authentication. "Why" is immediately evident; no one likes to receive too little for too much. "How" is a matter of careful training. You must learn to be consistently aware of the importance of buying from a reputable dealer. You must concentrate on the means of checking the originality of works in all media and by all artists. We shall discuss authentication methods in detail, and you will see that most of these depend chiefly on using a library. Many people fail to realize how valuable a library can be in answering the detailed questions that always accompany art collecting.

It is not difficult to learn how a gallery can help you identify a certain picture, what your legal position might be if you should buy something that is fraudulently misrepresented, and how you can decipher the collectors' marks that are often stamped on drawings, prints, and works in other media. Then, too, you should be thoroughly familiar with such terms as limited and unlimited editions, states, signed and numbered, artist proof, restrike, and estate signatures. Sound knowledge of all of these will allow you to decide with assurance whether or not what you are looking at and may eventually buy is both genuine and verifiable. Our discussion of the signature and the extent to which it determines the originality and significance of a work of art should dispel many popular misconceptions. Also, knowing how to identify indications of artist honor societies and other abbreviations that appear on graphics can sometimes save you money or enable you to understand more fully the background and authenticity of works on which these marks appear.

Armed with a firm knowledge of the various media and with a solid grasp of why and how to authenticate purchases, you will want to determine where to buy your fine art. There are many sources available to you, and most of them are accommodating and trustworthy; we shall stress the importance of dealing with a reputable concern, whether an art gallery, auction house, or antique store. Comparative shopping is absolutely necessary. An acquaintance with other important but perhaps lesser known practices, like home trials, commissions, and patronage, as well as with all of the publications listing national and international gallery offerings can also help you decide finally where to buy.

Tasteful framing and hanging are essential complements to all of your art purchases. An understanding of the frame's relation to the picture and to the environment in which it will "live" are the basis of proper framing. There are many guidelines to follow in selecting a framer and in acquiring novel framing ideas. Countless types of moldings are available on the market today. You should understand how to differentiate between them and how to decide which ones are most appropriate and correct for a given medium or style of art. There are, of course, many acceptable solutions to the framing problem of each picture, just as there are numerous display answers for every room. You can hang your art works in pairs or in any of many multiple arrangements. All of these groupings can be interesting, and all are a great deal of fun to organize.

The basic economic laws of supply and demand, changing styles and vogues, auction prices, subject matter, signatures, dates of execution, sales taxes, shipping, insurance, and even tax deductions are some of the factors governing the values, prices, and trends in art. A knowledge of all this is basic to the confidence you need for comparative shopping and eventual purchasing. In addition to the personal warmth and aesthetic satisfaction of collecting, you can also benefit from the monetary values of art works. Like many other salable commodities, they have resale values. They can be traded at any time like stocks and bonds, exchanged with or sold to a dealer or collector for current market prices. Anyone buying solely or partially for investment would probably be wise to collect old masters or important painters now in vogue, like Andrew Wyeth, Pablo Picasso, Marc Chagall, and Salvador Dali, along with some revived and some new names, whose prices continue to rise.

While collecting original art can be one of the most valuable experiences of your life, it is also within your means. Of course, originals afford innumerable advantages that photographic reproductions do not, the most significant of which is that your purchase was created directly by the hand of the artist. Then, too, no two original works of art are alike; whether you own oils, drawings, or graphics, yours are unique creations.

During the past few decades there has been a great resurgence of interest in the graphic media as significant modes of artistic expression. Lithographs, woodcuts, etchings, aquatints, and engravings are now universally collected. In fact, most major museums feature their print collections, and open periodic exhibitions of them to the public. Most private collectors recognize the graphic media as more than "art for the poor man's pocketbook," and important artists are increasingly attracted to graphic techniques because of the endless experimentation they encourage. Such renowned men as Maurice Utrillo, Pierre-Auguste Renoir, Georges Rouault (often called the greatest printmaker of the twentieth century), Pablo Picasso, Salvador Dali, Henry Moore, and such Americans as Raphael Soyer, John Taylor Arms, and Adolf Dehn are familiar names found in the print collections of your favorite art dealer. All are within the reach of the average family income and are bought today with enthusiasm. The future seems to hold even greater recognition of their already acclaimed graphic skills.

THE DISCOVERY

Collecting fine art can be great fun and as challenging an undertaking as you will ever pursue. Although the broad scope of the process should never be narrowed by the purchase of "big" names only, it is not unusual today for a work of art to be purchased for the single reason that the artist is a famous and important one. The unfortunate part of this procedure is, of course, that it leads to a disregard of the value of aesthetic expression. A work comes to be appreciated not for its artistic merit but for its function as a status symbol, as another way to "keep up with the Joneses." A well-planned collection is one that contains not only the presently favored popular artists but also reflects some daring experimentation with those who are less popular or unknown—artists whom you yourself like because their work intrigues, pleases, and satisfies you.

For centuries collectors have reaped the rewards and joys of discovering and collecting unknown artists, new styles and techniques, or other innovations. These collectors have gambled on the basis of predictions; they have tried to deduce the futures of artists they discover, forecasting who will eventually be "known" masters. If, as we emphasize, you keep up with gallery showings, you will have a fairly good idea of "who's who" on the current art scene. Some artists gain immediate favor after their initial showings; others may take longer. Once you know what is being shown, your tastes, predictions, and budget should be your guides, not just names that are already famous. One of the greatest satisfactions you can have as an art collector is to exhibit your own creativity by discovering an artist at just the right point in his career, immediately before his prices began to rise. Such discoveries are always possible.

AS THE ULTIMATE IN HOME DECORATION

Original works of art are unique in every respect; they convey impressions that are intimate, stimulating, and vital; they also lend a special flavor and character to the beauty of your home. We can even say that they are the ultimate in interior design—but not in the sense that they match and complement the color scheme of your rooms. They may by chance do this, but the fact remains that a work of art should first be appreciated and bought for its intrinsic aesthetic and visual delights—interior designers and decorators notwithstanding. One of the great mistakes new collectors can make is to try conscientiously to find a work of art that will match colors in a particular room. Some people even go so far as to carry rug or drapery samples with them while gallery visiting to see if they can "pick up" colors for their decorative schemes. This is unfortunate. Works of art are meant to speak for themselves. They should function independently in their own surroundings, and, because they are unique creations that will probably outlive man and his machine-produced wares, should take unquestioned precedence. If the home owner must coordinate his room with his art, then select the works of art first and carpets and upholstery later.

The question of purposely seeking colorful compositions as opposed to black and white subjects often arises in the minds of collectors. There is no permanent rule governing this consideration. Some of the most powerful compositions can be in black and white, whether they are drawings, lithographs, etchings, or any other media. Knowledgeable collectors consider black and white essential to a choice collection. A new collector can derive immense enjoyment from pen and pencil studies, preparatory works for more detailed or finished compositions. These drawings are becoming more and more popular today, and, as will be seen in Chapter 2, they are even regarded as a special class of collecting. Up-to-date connoisseurs are now appreciating these black and white subjects more than ever, and finding that they fit well with all other works in their collection. Understated studies, finished creations in black and white and in color, oils and graphics, ancient and modern can all work harmoniously to form a collection you can display both prominently and proudly.

Interest in art collecting has now reached an all-time high and shows no indication of declining. In the past few years, many factors have combined to stimulate our sophisticated and affluent society, so that we no longer consider art as limited to a select few. Advanced methods of transportation and communication have enabled us to become better informed and more highly educated. Our art consciousness has been further aroused by the construction of new museums and expansion of existing museum facilities, by art galleries, art magazines, documentary films, educational television, and art courses on the high school, college, and graduate levels. Today a variety of artistic media and a wide range of prices are available to persons seeking to own original art. Excellent quality drawings, paintings, graphics, and other media by established artists, their disciples, and new artists can be found to fit everyone's taste and budget. Long-term payment plans and credit-buying programs are now aiding many collectors.

There are no more capable art tutors than your own eyes and experiences. But you should expand upon your spontaneous reactions. Read as much as you can about art history, techniques, and other related subjects. This practice can be immeasurably satisfying and very rewarding. The books in the bibliography beginning on page 157 will all be useful to you. Above all, you must have patience, and from the very beginning direct yourself to collecting originals of the finest quality.

2 *Media and Techniques*

Honoré Daumier, lithograph.

ORIGINAL ART

An "original" work of art is one that comes directly from the hand of the artist. There are two varieties of the original—the single, one-of-a-kind original and the multiple original. Oils, pastels, temperas, drawings, watercolors, and gouaches are single one-of-a-kinds. The graphics—etchings, engravings, aquatints, drypoints, woodcuts, lithographs, and similar media—are multiple originals. To create an original oil painting the artist himself conceives the image and completes the work upon his canvas. In the graphic arts, the artist also creates his personal image, but works it upon stones, metal plates, or blocks of wood. From these a limited number of works are produced, each involving unique technical procedures and skills. Both forms of the original have been collected and prized for many centuries. Rembrandt's etchings were as widely collected by his contemporaries as were his oils. Picasso's lithographs are now as eagerly sought as his paintings and drawings.

In some instances in the past, artists excelled in one particular medium, or even in one form of the graphic arts, and did not work in any other. Honoré Daumier, the nineteenth-century French satirist, was almost exclusively a lithographer. Contemporary artists, on the other hand, often explore diverse media and may even exploit several techniques in a single work. We use the term painter-printmaker for an artist who works with both single and multiple originals.

OIL PAINTING

Credit for the invention of oil painting is traditionally given to the brothers Hubert and Jan van Eyck, the fifteenth-century Flemish masters. But aside from several works by Leonardo da Vinci, it was the Venetian painters—Giovanni Bellini (1430-1516), Titian (1485-1576), and others—who first exploited the full possibilities of working in oil and caused it to almost replace the previously favored fresco and tempera. Since then, one great school after another has advanced the oil technique, and today it remains one of the most popular forms of original art.

Oil paints are composed of colored vegetable or mineral powders mixed with oil, which is the binding substance. The paints are thick, and dry thick with the same consistency, but may be thinned by adding turpentine and benzene prior to application. Most contemporary oil painting is executed on stretched canvas; slate, marble, paper, paper on board, wood panels, copper, and

Maurice de Vlaminck, French. *Winter Landscape* (oil on canvas)
Collection of Mr. and Mrs. Harry G. Sundheim, Jr., Chicago, Illinois.

tin are other surfaces to which oils adhere. To apply oil paint the
artist uses either a brush or, as many contemporaries prefer, a
palette knife, a flat flexible-blade tool closely resembling a kitchen
knife. The artist may mix colors either on a palette before applying them to the canvas, or as he applies them, directly on the
painting surface. The latter method is called *alla prima*. Artists
may begin to paint without a strictly laid-out plan, or, as many of
the old masters did, they may make careful preparations on their
painting surfaces. The preparations might involve a detailed

Ernest Lawson, American. *The Old Tulip—Long Island Shore* (oil on canvas). Courtesy of James Graham & Sons, Inc., New York.

drawing or loosely painted forms on which color is eventually built. Often the artist lets his underpainting show through according to a prearranged scheme. When he does so, his total process of creation becomes part of our appreciation of the finished picture. As a final step, certain masters often use glazes, or transparent films of paint, to enhance the richness and luminosity of their work, and a coat of varnish both to protect their oils and to add a glossy finish.

As early as the sixteenth century, Titian and his followers developed the technique of impasto, the building up of layers of paint to add brilliance, texture, and three-dimensionality to paint

Milton Avery, American. *Summer Reader* (oil on canvas). Private collection.

surfaces. With its introduction, artists began to experiment extensively with the representation of light on canvas, which accounts for many of the varieties and subtleties of the oil medium. We can even say that in many respects impasto has been responsible for the unrivaled popularity of oil painting.

PASTEL

Pastels were first developed and popularly executed early in the eighteenth century. One of the first to experiment with them was the French master, Jean Baptiste Siméon Chardin. Unlike most other media except pencil drawing, pastel is a completely dry technique. In its earliest stages it involved the thin application of pastel chalks; these were gradually blended and rubbed, usually

Edgar Degas, French. *Rehearsal on the Stage* (pastel). The Metropolitan Museum of Art. Bequest of Mrs. H. O. Havemeyer, 1929. The H. O. Havemeyer collection.

with the fingers. Fragile, extremely delicate effects of surface and line were the result. During the eighteenth century, in fact, the exquisite finish and polish of pastels rivaled the effects of oils and watercolors, and it became common at this time to use pastels in place of oils. Pastel technique changed, however, during the nineteenth century. Whereas artists had formerly blended and rubbed the chalk, they now began to apply color within networks of lines, the effect of which is an arresting complication of surfaces.

One easy way to recognize pastels is to examine the papers on which they are drawn. Since the middle of the eighteenth century,

Mary Cassatt, American. *Ellen Mary Cassatt* (pastel). Courtesy of M. R. Schweitzer Gallery, New York.

many artists have been using tinted papers to help produce desired effects of light, shade, and depth. This was especially so in the works of Edgar Degas. In addition to color tint, the artist often selects textures of papers, either smooth or rough, to give texture to the pastel and structure to the drawing.

Probably the most fundamental characteristic that distinguishes pastels from other media is their prominent chalky smell, and their nonglossy, mat finish. Also often visible are traces of pencil with which artists begin their drawings, later accenting the drawn contours with their chalks. Most evident is the wide range of

Louis Legrand, French. *Petite Marcheuse* (crayon and pastel). Courtesy of James Graham & Sons, Inc.

pastel colors, varying from light and tinted hues to brilliant contrasts. The method of chalk application determines both color contrasts and surface textures. A soft, velvety, blended surface is obtainable in several ways, the most popular of which is cross-hatching, which Degas first developed fully. In this method, colors are first stroked at an angle and covered with a fixative to dry; then the second layer of colors is placed at an angle to the lower layer. These strokes are separate and distinct from those of the layers below.

Sometimes, rather than crosshatching, artists prefer to use parallel diagonals to obtain flat tones, modeling, and space. Corresponding colors in the spectrum give brilliant effects when juxtaposed. Orange, for example, is more brilliant when next to yellow. This is the intriguing quality of pastels. They can be soft and subtle, or by contrast of color they can be brilliant.

Because pastels never adhere permanently to the surface of the paper, you should handle them carefully. Glass or a variety of fixatives are most often used to protect them. Adverse chemical reactions of fixatives may, however, change the original tones of the pastel. For this reason, glass is usually the best protection.

Pastel drawings are more in demand today than ever. Some are slight, and suggest much more than they state; others are highly finished works of art. Pastel drawings that merely hint at the subject matter seem to be most attractive to collectors. Studies of a head, or of hands, or of an unfinished nude are much in vogue, and we will discuss these later at more length.

TEMPERA

History tells us that tempera, the medium used by the ancient Egyptians, is the oldest form of painting. A binding colloidal or gelatinous material is necessary to make tempera paint. Over the centuries, artists working in this very difficult medium have come to use egg yolks as the binding substance. Today's technique, which also utilizes egg yolks, is a direct, quick-drying process frequently favored for sketch work. Like pastel, tempera has been revived during the last twenty years. Its decline before this time was, of course, due to the popularity of the more fluid oil painting.

Tempera paints have body like oils but are more predominately

Andrew Wyeth, American. *A Crow Flew By* (tempera on wood). The Metropolitan Museum of Art, Arthur H. Hearn Fund, 1950.

translucent. Color is of paramount importance. Generally, *white* is the solid background of tempera paintings, since it functions as light and is the neutral against which the colors of the spectrum are blended. Unlike oils, which are mixed colors, tempera colors are usually pure. The artist generally blends them directly on his surface, not on the palette. He blends them horizontally or vertically, often with crosshatching so that you can see colors of one layer combined with those of layers beneath. You can always detect the brush strokes, which delineate soft, subtle modeling and tones. Sketches or drawings, which are the artist's notes about placement and color, usually accompany the tempera painting. Andrew Wyeth, the great contemporary American, may use twenty or thirty sketches in preparation for his final tempera rendition.

Many artists execute temperas on cardboard or wooden panels, which often are more helpful than absorbent canvases in achieving smoothness and richness. Also, the hard immobile surfaces of cardboard and wooden panels are less liable to crack than canvas. Tempera very rarely reflects light and is therefore one of the best media for photographic reproduction. For the artist, it is a tedious and demanding medium; what an oil painter can do in an hour might take a tempera painter weeks to accomplish. Testimony to the permanence and resiliency of tempera is the splendid condition of the works by Italian masters of the thirteenth and fourteenth centuries, including Giotto's thirteenth century *Madonna and Child Enthroned* in the Uffizi Gallery in Florence.

DRAWING

Drawn contours, outlines, and isolated marks distinguish our earliest pictorial images, those eloquent statements by prehistoric man. Drawing continues to be the truest record of the artist's thought, imagination, and personality. What he will say in his finished oil is first stated, very likely with greater candor, in the preliminary drawing.

Drawings are usually executed in pen or pencil, or the two combined. Artists often heighten or accent the features of a drawing with colored ink or sepia, a kind of warm brownish tone ink. A coat of wash or water over a drawing makes it appear spontaneous, luminous, and transparent, much like a watercolor. Sepia affords extraordinary effects of light and atmosphere. Drawings may be rendered on any kind of paper—old or new, tinted or plain, sometimes even on hotel stationery, newspaper, napkins, or any surface able to retain pencil lead or ink.

You will find that good original drawings have movement, compositional order, a sense of depth, and an accomplished de-

Joseph-Louis-Hippolyte Bellangé, French. *Seated Musketeer* (pen and ink drawing). Courtesy of The Drawing Shop, New York.

gree of modeling. The rhythm and tempo possessed by drawings is exceedingly different from that of the graphic or painted arts. They may subtly suggest more than is actually stated, or may lend an alluring animation to forms through precise and penetrating detail. When drawings are studies for oils, they should have many of the characteristics of the finished oil. The drawings of Jan van Goyen, a sixteenth century Dutch master, have, for example, the same lush atmospheric quality as his oils. An artist seeks to delin-

Eugène Delacroix, French. *Algerian Heads* (pen and ink drawing). Collection of Mr. and Mrs. Raphael Soyer.

eate the essentials of his form and action, and in this endeavor he may do thirty or forty drawing studies for an oil painting. Since in a drawing the artist is working out problems and laying the foundations for his finished product, distortion and exaggeration are not uncommon. It is not surprising that modern collectors are now seeking drawings with these qualities, for they reflect the free

Henri Edmond Cross, French. *Flute Player* (pencil draw-ing). Courtesy of M. R. Schweitzer Gallery, New York.

creative process of the artist and show the path he has followed toward his final conception.

Though collecting drawings was secondary at the turn of the century, today it is "the thing to do." People now appreciate the thought, meaning, and decorative attributes of these works. For-tunately, however, the contemporary market for drawings is not

Léon Lhermitte, French. *Study of a Young Peasant Girl* (pen and ink drawing). Collection of Mrs. Jeffrey H. Loria.

yet as desperately competitive as the markets for some other media. People are just now beginning to collect drawings, and the supply has not yet been offset by the demand. In the next ten years, however, this situation is likely to be reversed.

WATERCOLOR

Most people think of Albrecht Dürer, the great fifteenth century German artist, as an engraver and woodcutter of supreme talent and vision. Few of us realize, however, that watercolor and gouache were the media he first learned to use, and that his watercolors alone would have assured him a permanent place in the history of art. From Dürer's Germany, where it was first developed, the watercolor technique spread to The Netherlands and then to the rest of the Continent. It was not until the nineteenth century, however, that patronage of the watercolor flourished in England. During this period such English masters as J.M.W.

John Singleton Copley, American. *Two Soldiers* (pencil drawing).
Collection of Mr. and Mrs. Vincent Price, Los Angeles, California.

Turner, William Callow, and Peter DeWint produced distinctive
and picturesque works of art in watercolor. Yet, despite even
these achievements, prior to the 1930's American art patrons
considered watercolor a minor offshoot of oil painting. Today,
though, collectors finally appreciate the technical facility watercolors must have in order to create the most fundamental image.

To produce the watercolor, a pigment is ground in gum—
generally gum arabic—and applied with a brush and water to
paper. Watercolors are transparent; you can thus differentiate
them from the more widely used, thicker oils. An oil painter produces his "whites" and light with impasto, or layers of paint, but
the watercolor artist usually does so by letting you see the white
of his paper. John Singer Sargent was a master of this device. In a

Raphael Soyer, American. *Two Heads*
(pencil drawing). Private collection.

sense, the subtlety of the watercolorist's art lies in his leaving out
much of what the oil painter might amplify.

Good watercolors are fluid and fresh; their composition holds a
special delight for the viewer. You can usually distinguish the
range of a single color within one watercolor. One shade or many
shades can be derived from a single color, depending on the
amount of water added to the primary color. For instance, if
cobalt blue, a deep blue, is strongly thinned with water, it will
become a soft blue. In addition, special atmospheric effects and
textures are often achieved by wetting the paper before beginning
work, or by applying the watercolor with a sponge or razor blade.

Artists often draw their compositions in pencil before applying watercolor. Pencil marks are, therefore, often visible beneath the surface of the watercolor; these in no way detract from the finished work but present an interesting linear contrast to the sensitive washes of color. While watercolors can be executed on almost

Charles Demuth, American. *Green Pears* (watercolor). Courtesy of Yale University Art Gallery.

any paper, rag papers of varying weights are best. The ability to recognize heavy rag papers ranging from fifty or sixty to two hundred fifty pound weight will help you distinguish original watercolors from facsimiles, usually rendered on a less textured, lighter paper.

The greatest virtuoso of watercolor was Winslow Homer, who is often said to be responsible for making the watercolor as distinguished and readily accepted as the oil painting. The exquisite articulation and monumentality of his early watercolors are all the more admirable when we realize that this medium is one of the most difficult an artist can use. To attain the spontaneous quality of a good watercolor, the first image must be essentially true, for compositions in this medium are hard to change. As a rule the artist must try many times before completing a watercolor that meets his expectations. Yet, like drawing, the watercolor is a

John Singer Sargent, American. *Temple in a Garden* (watercolor). Collection of Mr. and Mrs. Howard Aberg, Arlington, Virginia.

medium that artists often use to execute major studies for important oil canvases.

GOUACHE

Though the gouache is becoming a favorite medium of modern artists, it is in no way a modern medium. Its name was derived from the old Italian word *guazzo,* and it has been used by artists for several centuries. A gouache is essentially a quick-drying,

Winslow Homer, American. *Hurricane, Bahamas* (watercolor). The
Metropolitan Museum of Art, Lazarus Fund, 1910.

opaque watercolor containing a special filler. The colors contain
the same ingredients as watercolors, plus inert pigments that give
a heavier and stronger appearance. Unlike the watercolors which
should be executed quickly and without change, fast-drying gouache
is an easy medium to handle.

Gouache, unlike the transparent watercolor, has a paint quality
produced by the thickness of the medium. A coat of varnish is
often used over its fiberlike surface to enhance color intensity and
enliven dark colors. Vivacity, freshness of color, and direct execution are the most easily recognizable qualities of this medium. If,
however, the work lacks organization and development of form,
spontaneity can become sloppiness. You must judge whether an

Vincent Capraro, American. *The Prophet* (watercolor).
Private collection.

original gouache achieves a successful balance of spontaneity and
organization.

The amount of white paint used and the degree of color intensity added to the opaque medium of a gouache determine the
liveliness of color. Like oils, texture is paramount for gouache;
the three-dimensional layers of pigment enable you to see all of
the steps that have led to the completed picture. Since the medium
dries quickly, the artist can work and rework the composition and

achieve varied, unusual textures. Because of its versatility, he often uses the gouache for experimentation and invention. In many instances the steps leading to creation of an oil painting include a drawing and a gouache. Gouaches originally used as sketch preparations are widely collected and highly prized. Yasuo

Milton Avery, American. *Surf Watchers* (watercolor). Courtesy of Mrs. Milton Avery.

Kuniyoshi, Adolf Dehn, Marc Chagall, Mark Tobey, and Ben Shahn are well known for their gouaches, which reflect the spontaneity of their brush strokes.

MIXED MEDIA

Many artists combine oils, watercolors, pencil, pastel, and india ink—or any combination—within a single composition, often using guide lines for the drawing beneath. For instance, you will

Eugene Berman, American. *L'Opéra* (gouache). Courtesy of Sears, Roebuck and Co., The Vincent Price Collection.

often see drawings heightened with watercolor and further accented by colored chalks or gouache. Joan Miró, the renowned contemporary Spanish artist, often mixes chalks, crayon, pencil, and ink. His mixed-media compositions and those of many other contemporary artists are collected avidly.

GRAPHIC ART

Graphic art was first produced early in the fifteenth century. Because graphics are multiple originals, they have been more extensively distributed and easily secured than one-of-a-kinds. Today, graphic prints are the most widely collected forms of original art. They are available at prices from a few to thousands of dollars.

Byron Browne, American. *Crustacean Icon* (gouache). Courtesy of Mrs. Byron Browne, New York.

THE PRINT

The beginning collector may misunderstand the term print. Be careful not to confuse its two popular uses: "print" as referring to original graphic art, and "print" as designating photographic reproductions. Prints that are lithographs, etchings, engravings, woodcuts, aquatints, and drypoints differ from photographic prints. In the former techniques the artist himself does all of the work on the stone, the plate, or the wood block. Since the entire execution comes directly from his hand, the work is unique and wholly original. Conversely, the artist has nothing to do with, and often does not approve of, photographically reproduced prints.

Jules Pascin, American. *Two Figures* (mixed media).
Collection of Mr. and Mrs. Raphael Soyer, New York.

THE "RARE" PRINT

As a collector of fine prints, you should have in mind the meaning
of the word rare. Generally, an art dealer using this qualifier in
conversation means that there exist only about twenty or so examples of the etching or lithograph to which he is referring. For
some artists, however, rare can signify even fewer examples. With
Degas, for instance, it usually means that only two or three impressions exist. Artists often make impressions for themselves

Pablo Picasso, Spanish. *Max Jacob* (etching). Private collection.

without intending to distribute them publicly. Sometimes, though, these prints find their way into the market; they, too, are rare prints, whether signed or unsigned.

ETCHING

Etching, one of the most popular forms of graphic art, originated in northern Europe during the early sixteenth century. Essentially, the process requires that the artist cover a metal or copper plate with a coat of wax, and draw directly on the plate by cutting through the wax with an etching needle. He then submerges or dips the plate into an acid bath. The acid "bites" or eats into the

Pablo Picasso, Spanish. *Two Nudes*
(etching). Courtesy of A. Lublin, Inc.,
New York.

metal along the lines drawn with the etching needle, and causes
furrows or grooves to appear in the metal. Successive bitings in an
acid bath determine the thinness or thickness of the bitten line.
Artists usually have to submerge the plate more than once to
achieve the desired effects of light, shade, and accent.

After the acid baths, the artist removes the wax from the plate.
Then he files the rim to a smooth finish, so as not to tear the paper
during printing. To print, the artist covers the plate with ink,
which runs into the etched furrows. He then wipes the surface
clean and, using a simple hand press, affixes a dampened piece of
paper to the plate. In this way, the drawing on the plate is transferred to the paper. Note that the transfer is in reverse; when you
look at an etching or other form of printed graphic, you look at

Marc Chagall, Russian. From *The Bible Series* (etching, hand colored by the artist). Courtesy of Sears,
Roebuck and Co., The Vincent Price Collection.

the reverse of the composition actually drawn on the plate.

Most etchings are black and white, but some artists work with
colors, each of which requires an extra printing. In other words, if
the two colors of an etching are red and blue, the artist first inks
the appropriate section of the plate with red ink and prints it; he
then cleans the surface, inks the section intended to be blue, and
prints again in a similar fashion.

Contemporary etchings are most often rendered on old hand-

Details, much enlarged, showing the sort of lines made by the etching
needle. From an etching, *Calvary Church in Snow*, by Childe Hassam.
Photograph courtesy of Norman Jackson.

made Dutch, French, or Japanese paper. These papers, sometimes
more than one hundred years old, are generally very soft and
pliable. Artists prefer old papers because they enhance the etching's richness, beauty, and warmth of tone. Also, old papers are
devoid of the modern chemicals that can fade and discolor etchings, whether they are black and white or multicolored.

You can easily recognize original etchings by the rigid plate
marks on the outermost edges of the paper. These appear as
heightened and embossed edges surrounding the etching. If etchings are offered to you framed, be sure that this important characteristic is visible for your study. A facsimile of the plate mark is

Another enlargement of lines made by the etching needle. From *Les petites têtes d'hommes coiffées à l'orientale*, by G. B. Castiglione. Photograph courtesy of Norman Jackson.

often produced photographically on reproductions. Two things will help you distinguish originals from facsimiles: first, feeling whether the plate mark is smooth and therefore photographed, or raised and therefore original; and second, noting whether the plate mark is visible from the *reverse side* of the paper, which is possible only on originals.

The characteristic etched line does not decrease or increase in successive graduated stages. Its end is square, abrupt, and untapered. Learn to understand its coarse texture and raised quality by gently running your fingertip over the etching. Always remember that the lines of the etcher's needle achieve all the effects

Detail, much enlarged, from an engraving by Hendrik
Goltzius, showing the scooped line of the burin. Photograph courtesy of Norman Jackson.

of the composition, whether they are forms, or figures, or subtle
tones of shadow.

ENGRAVING

Engraving originated in the mid-fifteenth century. At that time
the craftsmen of northern Europe used to cut lines, forms, and

William Hogarth, English. Street scene (no title)—engraving. Collection of Mr. Eugene Santomasso, New York.

designs on wood, metal, and gold. Now, in a similar way, the engraver draws a composition on a metal plate by cutting lines or furrows with a burin, a small steel rod with a triangularly pointed end that is set at an oblique angle. This process is exceedingly slow, for the burin must scoop or cut deeply into the metal, not just scratch the surface, as with etchings, on which the acid actually does the cutting.

The cut of the burin produces sharp and crisp lines. Whereas

Jack Levine, American. *Small Face*
(copper engraving). Courtesy A.
Lublin, Inc., New York.

etched lines end abruptly, engraved lines taper gradually. This is
because the amount of pressure placed on the burin can cause the
width of the line to vary. Generally, engraved lines are thinnest at
the end. Moreover, the finished composition of an engraving is
not usually as free-flowing as that of the etching. A needle on wax
can produce a line instantly, with only light scratching, and glides
across the surface of the metal at the will of the artist. The engraver, however, must dig through the metal in a slower, more
deliberate manner.

Engravings are printed much like etchings. The artist inks the
furrows of the cut lines. He then dampens a piece of paper with

Detail, much enlarged, from an aquatint, #5, Goya's *Disasters of War* series, showing mottled tones and lines in combination. Photograph courtesy of Norman Jackson.

warm water, places it above the inked metal plate, and runs them both through a simple hand press. As with the etching, the image is in reverse, and you can see a rigid plate mark around the four edges of the engraving. The embossed edges are also visible from the reverse side of the engraving.

Artists very often use engraving to complete areas of an etching already started. In fact, the two processes are frequently combined, and it is often difficult even for the experts to see which lines on a composition were etched and which engraved.

Georges Rouault, French. *Head of Christ* (aquatint).
Courtesy of Yale University Art Gallery.

AQUATINT

The aquatint technique, invented during the eighteenth century, is
essentially a tonal process based upon the action of a resin that
the artist delicately filters over the surface of an etched or engraved plate. By heating the plate and dipping it into an acid
bath, he causes the surface on which the resin has been placed to
become granulated, covered with tiny holes. Then, inking the

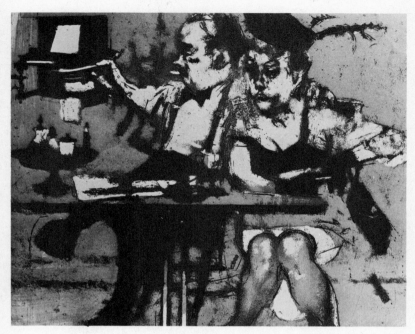

Jack Levine, American. *Love, Careless Love* (aquatint). Private collection.

plate and printing from it, he creates a composition that combines the lines of the etching or engraving with the mottled tones of the aquatint. These tones vary according to the depths to which the different portions of the plate are bitten, and can reveal gradations from black to gray to white. The tones are characteristically opaque and often cause the aquatint area of the work to resemble a flat piece of hammered antique silver. The effects of etching and engraving are created by lines; tone, shadow, and masses create those of the aquatint. These different media are, however, very often combined, and when we say aquatint we usually mean aquatint over engraving or etching. The aquatint rarely appears alone. When placing it over another medium, an artist is said to

Detail, much enlarged, from a drypoint by Huc-
Mazelet Luquiens, showing the dry scratched
line. Photograph courtesy of Norman Jackson.

be "combining techniques."

Francisco Goya, the eighteenth century Spaniard, was the supreme master of the aquatint. He first made etchings and then
added aquatints to them. The granulated surface that resulted
gives the light and atmosphere of his aquatints a vibrant quality
impossible to achieve with any other medium. Today printmakers
are again turning to the aquatint as an adjunct to etching and
engraving. Georges Rouault, the master twentieth century French
painter and printmaker, executed many aquatints, some of the

Mary Cassatt, American. *Sara* (drypoint). Private collection.

best examples of which are in the permanent print collection of the Museum of Modern Art in New York.

DRYPOINT

Drypoint, which resembles engraving and etching, was first executed in Germany in the late fifteenth century. Whereas the etching is the product of the acid-bitten line, the drypoint is the result of the dry, scratched line.

To create a drypoint the artist sketches directly on a bare piece of metal. He uses a needle having a steel tip set with a diamond, ruby, or other hard precious stone. The needle scratches the surface of the metal and leaves an identifiable, irregular ridge on

Detail, much enlarged, from woodcut, *St. Christopher*, by Albrecht Dürer. All except the black lines have been cut away from the wood block. Photograph courtesy of Norman Jackson.

either side of every line. This ridged line is either saw-edged, razor-edged, or knife-edged, depending upon the direction of the drypoint and the pressure put on it. The printing of the drypoint is similar to that of etchings and engravings. The metal plate is printed in reverse on a simple hand press.

You can recognize the drypoint line by its rich, velvety feeling, by a softness which the etched acid-bitten line and the burin lines of the engraving cannot capture. Like the aquatint, the drypoint is often an adjunct to etching. You will find that some compositions combine all three techniques—the etching defined further by the drypoint and heightened by the aquatint.

Mervin Jules, American. *Duo* (woodcut, two states). (*Left*) an early block; (*right*) a later proof with several blocks.

WOODCUTTING

The woodcut was the earliest graphic process. Its potentials were first exploited in China during the T'ang dynasty of the eighth century and in Europe during the early fifteenth century by Dürer, the earliest European master to work with the woodcut. Following him were the "little masters," Pencz, Beham, and Altdorfer, who portrayed religious scenes and vignettes from everyday life. The woodcut continued to be important for artists until the nineteenth century, but at that time it was rivaled by the newly introduced daguerreotype. The color woodcuts produced in Japan and China during the latter part of the nineteenth century greatly influenced contemporary development of the technique. During the twentieth century, along with the very similar and recently developed linoleum or linocut technique, the woodcut has again become a major form of graphic art. Leonard Baskin and Antonio Frasconi are two chief contemporary exponents of the woodcut; Henri Matisse and Pablo Picasso, aside from their work in lithography, have also furthered the technique of the linocut. Original woodcuts differ markedly from lithographs, etchings, and engravings. The woodcut is a relief process; the others involve an intaglio method, which means that the drawn lines are incised or engraved. The woodcut is very simple to print, and requires only a hand roller press. The woodcutter first draws directly on the surface of the wood block, which is usually cherry wood, seven-eighths of an inch thick. He uses burins, gouges, chisels, and other special tools to cut away the wood with the grain and raise his composition in relief on the block. The design areas that are left in relief are called the "black" or positive areas; those areas around the design that are cut away are the "white" or negative areas.

After cutting, the artist inks the wood block with either black or colored ink. If the woodcut is to have more than one color, he must make an additional block for each color. The pigments for

Leonard Baskin, American. *Head of Eakins* (woodcut). Private collection.

colored woodcuts are ground in water and applied to the block like a paste.

Black and white woodcuts are most easily identified by the interplay of solid areas of blacks and whites. Woodcuts present form in silhouette. You can feel a variety of textures by touching them. These textures, from the grain of the wood, are an integral part of the artistic expression.

The hand-printed woodcut is most often rendered on white Japanese rice paper, which you can recognize by the watermark lines that are approximately three-quarters of an inch apart over

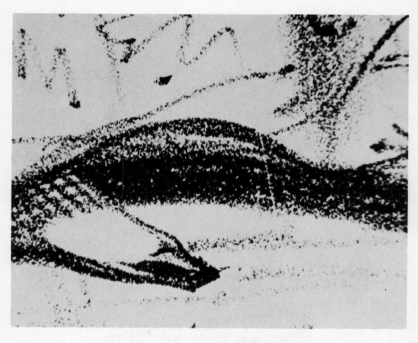

Detail, much enlarged, from a lithograph by Gavarni, showing the
soft, waxy line. Photograph courtesy of Norman Jackson.

the whole surface. This paper retains color pigments whose pene-
tration you can see from the reverse side of the composition. The
color is not only a surface effect but also part of the paper.

An additional way to recognize the color woodcut is by its
color gradation, which is determined by the amount of pigment
and water applied to the thin rice paper. Become familiar with
this richness of color. When an original color woodcut is held to
the light its shading should be deepened and enhanced. You
should examine a woodcut in both artificial light and daylight,
since it will look different in each. See it, too, in the position in
which it will be hung on your wall.

Auguste Renoir, French. *Louis Valtat* (lithograph).
Courtesy of A. Lublin, Inc., New York.

LITHOGRAPHY

The lithograph originated in Bavaria in 1798 with the unique
discovery by Aloys Senefelder that grease and water do not mix.
"Lithograph" comes from the Greek words *lithos,* stone, and
graphein, to write. To execute a lithograph, the artist draws his
composition directly on a prepared slab of porous limestone with
crayons which contain a resin or a wax. He then applies ink,
which adheres only to the places covered with the crayon. To

Henri de Toulouse-Lautrec, French. *The Chestnut Vendor* (lithograph). Collection of Mrs. Stanley Weinstein, Fairfield, Connecticut.

print, he usually works with a professional skilled in the complicated process of "pulling" or printing lithographs. The lithographer will clean the stone with acid and water prior to each pull.

At the beginning of the nineteenth century, the French masters Eugène Delacroix, Theodore Géricault, and Eugène Isabey began a great tradition of the painter-lithographer. When photography was introduced in the mid-nineteenth century, however, lithogra-

Marino Marini, Italian. *Cavalier sur fond beige* (color lithograph). Courtesy of Yale University Art Gallery.

phy declined. It was revitalized by the Impressionists in the 1870's and 1880's. Degas, Manet, Pissarro, and finally Toulouse-Lautrec in the 1890's brought about an unprecedented revival. Lithography developed appreciably in America in the early decades of the twentieth century, especially through the work of Joseph Pennell, Adolf Dehn, George Bellows, Raphael Soyer, Thomas Hart Benton, and Stow Wengenroth. The tremendous contemporary interest in collecting lithographs results largely from the work of the School of Paris from 1940 to the present. Braque, Picasso, Chagall, Léger, Rouault, Matisse, Moore, Severini, and others,

Salvador Dali, Spanish. *The Mystical Rose Madonna* (lithograph). Courtesy of Sears, Roebuck and Co., The Vincent Price Collection.

along with American artists, have developed lithography into an art form that rivals oil paintings in appeal and popularity. The Tamarind Lithography Workshop in Los Angeles, California, under the direction of Mrs. June C. Wayne, has been in great measure responsible for the recent resurgence of interest in American lithography.

If you see a lithograph stone in any museum and then see an original lithograph printed from it, you will find that the vividness and spontaneity of the drawing on the stone is always transferred to the print. This liveliness can never be achieved by photographic reproduction, and is a distinguishing trait. You can also find the mark of the outer edge of the lithograph stone around the edge of the printed lithograph. It is not as distinguishable as the plate mark of an etching, but certainly its slightly suggested presence can help you discern the original. Contemporary lithographs are generally rendered on *Arches* paper or *Rives* paper, heavy papers having a textured grain. You can often distinguish their watermarks by holding the paper up to light. The printed words *Arches* or *Rives* will then be visible. During printing, the grain in all of the area pressed by the lithograph stone is flattened. You can always look for the juxtaposition of the flattened and the regularly grained paper. Look, too, for some slight relief or raising of color above the surface of the paper. This is usually good evidence of an original.

You can usually distinguish lithographs by an inklike odor almost always present, even years after printing. Also, original lithographs have subtle and widely-ranged tones and textures never captured in mechanical reproductions. No method can duplicate the deep blacks and intense, rich colors of hand-printed original lithographs.

3   *Authentication*

Honoré Daumier, lithograph.

Your art purchases should be ones that you like and that you know to be authentic. Whereas liking depends on your own tastes, determining authenticity is a matter of objective knowledge. Your sense of taste activates itself spontaneously the minute you look at a picture, but your awareness of a possible art abuse comes only with training and learning. The two most important criteria for purchasing a work of art are that you like it and that you are sure it is genuine. In establishing these standards your taste, knowledge, and resourcefulness are all very important. Taste is a personal matter that may or may not be logically justified. The procedure of establishing the authenticity of a certain work, on the contrary, may be easily learned.

ABUSES IN GRAPHIC ART

Abuses in graphic art take many forms. Photographic illustrations, textbook illustrations taken from old books and made to look even older by some chemical tampering with the paper on which they appear, and restrikes from canceled plates, often beautifully mounted and framed, may be offered to you as "originals." This is not always done willfully. Dealers who are unfamiliar with the history of art or with the art market may, without even realizing it, sell "bad" drawings and prints. Always inquire about the man with whom you are dealing; ask some collector friends, gallery owners, artists, or your local museum—all of whom will answer with a keen interest and sense of responsibility if you show them your enthusiasm. And, when making a purchase always insist that the dealer give you a written guarantee stipulating the authenticity of the work acquired; this is for your own future safety.

Count on your instincts, too. The public has proved itself a better judge of art than you might guess. In fact, a gallery that opened on Madison Avenue in New York in 1959, and tried to sell fraudulent copies of contemporary paintings and prints had no takers at all during the ten short months of its existence. This gallery finally had to admit to the discerning art public that it would no longer try to offer its bogus "Picassos" and "Braques."

THE BARGAIN

As interest in art collecting has increased during the past ten years, many dishonest operators have appeared. Some offer to sell original lithographs or etchings at unbelievably low prices. The Better Business Bureau claims that in most cases this art consists of inexpensive reproductions. If you encounter an art seller of questionable reputation, stay absolutely clear of the bargain. Always remember that, like Wall Street stocks, the established artists have market prices. There is no such thing as a real bargain. A work priced much lower than other examples on the market by the same artist is probably not authentic. Similarly, if you buy from an art dealer who claims to be "forced by circumstances" to sell out as quickly as possible, you may well be duped by what at first appeared to be a real bargain, and you will probably find later that the dealer has moved and left no forwarding address.

To protect yourself against a possible encounter with one of the few dishonest galleries that exist, and perhaps against an irresistible instinct that prompts you to purchase an art bargain, you should learn—and it is not difficult—how to do your own verifying.

MUSEUM STUDY

One excellent way to protect yourself from purchasing copies and fraudulent works is to become familiar with museum originals. College museums are often helpful in this regard, especially if you are far from a large city. Suppose, for example, you are interested in a Pissarro drawing. Generally, an original Pissarro has a spontaneous quality that a forged one will probably lack. Awkwardness, stiffness, lack of precision, and even haphazard organization are some of the shortcomings of the fake you can see for yourself if you are familiar with certified museum originals of other drawings by the same artist. This is what is meant by developing "an eye" for the original. Indeed, one of the greatest satisfactions you can have as a collector is to recognize upon first sight that something has been represented to you incorrectly.

LIBRARY STUDY

Unquestionably, the best sources of verification available to the established collector as well as the aspiring novice are the thousands of public, private, and museum libraries throughout the country. For the most part these are easily accessible, generously stocked, and well staffed. It is probably best to start at the shelves labeled "Art Reference." According to the Dewey Decimal System these are in the 700's. Until the early 1940's these sections were frequented most by scholars, who used the books to study the stylistic development of selected artists, rather than for verification of their works. Recently, however, and simultaneous with the increased interest in buying art, many other art lovers and collectors, regardless of their levels of education, consult the art-reference sections. Many want to know more about a contemplated purchase, others about works they already own.

GENERAL REFERENCE BOOKS

One of the most informative general-reference books is Bryan's *Dictionary of Painters and Engravers*. Found in almost every library, this series records all important artists of every nationality from the beginning of the history of art to the early twentieth century. The listings are arranged alphabetically by artist, and give his school, his birth and death dates, some description of his style, and in many instances a list of his prizes and of the museum collections in which he is represented. Another reference series, Benezit's *Dictionnaire des Peintres, Sculpteurs, Dessinateurs et Graveurs* records all known signatures for many of the major artists. Benezit, like Bryan, is excellent to help you recognize and become more familiar with the work of a particular artist. Then, too, the collector who has everything may aspire to find a fine work by an artist who is "not in Benezit."

SPECIALIZED REFERENCE BOOKS

There are numbers of outstanding specialized books that deal with individual artists and their entire body of work or *oeuvre*. Internationally recognized art critics and historians have compiled these specific references for some of the major artists. Many of these catalogue only the graphic work of the artists who are in vogue today and appear regularly in the art market. It is their graphic art that is now most widely collected because it is within the means of the average collector and more available than

one-of-a-kind oils, watercolors, pastels, temperas, and drawings.
Specialized reference books catalogue the work of the old masters of the Dutch and German schools of the fifteenth and sixteenth centuries; the celebrated Goya, Piranesi, and Rembrandt;
masters in the seventeenth and eighteenth centuries; the ever-
popular nineteenth-century French artists like Corot; the great
contemporary European printmakers like Picasso and Braque;
the colorful and subtle Orientals; and others. These complete
compilations are sometimes referred to as *catalogues raisonnés*—
complete résumés of an individual artist's *oeuvre*. In many cases
they contain illustrations of the most important examples listed.

SPECIALIZED REFERENCE BOOK: REMBRANDT

One of the best of these specialized books is Arthur Mayger
Hind's *Rembrandt's Etchings*. In it you will find a great deal of
information about Rembrandt's recorded etchings. If you happen
to be considering the purchase of one, you will undoubtedly want
to know, for example, when it was originally executed; whether or
not it was signed or dated, or both; its measurements; the number
of "states" it had during its evolution to a full and complete work;
and the exact differences between those recorded states.

THE STATE OF THE PRINT

The state of an etching, engraving, lithograph, or woodcut refers
to the specific number of alterations made by the artist on a single
etched plate, lithograph stone, or wood block. Some artists are
completely satisfied on the first printing; the resultant work therefore has only one recorded state. The numbered editions found on
today's art market are, for example, the first and only states executed. Hind tells us, however, that the etching *The Great Jewish
Bride* has *four* recorded states. In its first state the dress of the
figure and the lower part of the etched plate are left white, and
neither signature nor date appears. After the pull of this state

Rembrandt decided to alter the arms, dress, and background behind the figure with a rather heavy elaboration. He therefore
worked the plate again; hence, the second state, which also is the
state in which he signed the etching (in reverse) and dated it
(1635). Studying the plate again, however, Rembrandt had still
another idea for improvement, and in the third state he added
crosslines of shading to the hands of the figure. In the fourth, and
last state, he accented the architecture to the right by dividing the
stonework with horizontal lines.

In most cases the earlier states of old master etchings are more
valuable and costly. Today, however, with most of the early states
located in permanent museum collections, you should be more
than happy to own third- or fourth-state etchings. These are indeed collectors' items and many of them are rare jewels of art. If,
though, you are told in an offhand way that an etching you are
considering buying is the fourth state of six, verify this fact in
Hind's book or in Richard Munz's *Rembrandt's Etchings,* another
text written by an eminent Rembrandt scholar. You may discover
that the etching is known to have had only three recorded states.
If so, we suggest that you leave it and search elsewhere. Of
course, the dealer may himself offer to use some recognized
recorded books from his own library to explain the history of the
work in question. If so, he probably has nothing to hide and is
well versed in his field. You will find, too, that many dealers have
files and catalogues of previous collections and exhibitions that
the work has been in, copies of books and diaries in which the
work has been mentioned, or other similar means of authentication.* For maximum assurance, however, standard reference
texts should be your first criterion.

* One diary is that of the American painter Robert Henri, one of the famous
members of the Ashcan School, who not only recorded all of his oils by their
dates and the exhibitions at which they were shown, but also signed his paintings
on the reverse side of the canvas and numbered them to correspond with his
diary. The great Hudson River School painter, Eastman Johnson, was also
known to have kept a diary and recorded his oils in a similar fashion.

Rembrandt, Dutch. *The Great Jewish Bride* (etching, first state). The Metropolitan Museum of Art. Bequest of Mrs. H. O. Havemeyer, 1929. The H. O. Havemeyer collection.

Rembrandt, Dutch. *The Great Jewish Bride* (etching, fourth state). Courtesy of Yale University Art Gallery.

Rembrandt, Dutch. *The Three Crosses* (etching, second state).
The Metropolitan Museum of Art, gift of Felix M. Warburg
and his family, 1941.

CLIPPING MARGINS

Another useful fact learned by library study is that it was an
established practice in Rembrandt's day to clip the margins of the
paper very close to the outer edges of the etching. Most of the
etchings worked by Rembrandt himself were closely clipped in
this way. Such a characteristic should help you distinguish the
originals from the impressions made in the nineteenth century,
which usually have wide margins. The nineteenth-century prints
come from the original plates and do have market value, though
they are understandably less valuable than the originals.

Rembrandt, Dutch. *The Three Crosses* (etching, fourth state).
The Metropolitan Museum of Art, gift of Felix M. Warburg
and his family, 1941.

FACSIMILES

There are also worthless facsimiles of Rembrandt's work. The
most famous of these reproductions were made by Amand
Durand (1831-1905), the famous French heliographer and editor. You can easily identify his facsimiles, executed in the 1880's
and 1890's, by the Amand Durand monogram on the back of the
print. The same editor also made photographic facsimiles of Van
Dyck, Dürer, Ostade, and Claude Lorrain.

COPIES

Artists of Rembrandt's caliber have, over the centuries, been
copied. Though a copied etching naturally lacks the quality of the

original, it is often difficult to detect one, especially without a second etching for comparison. There are many nineteenth century copies that have fooled even the experts and the difficulty of discerning the difference should alert you even more to the value of reference sources for authentication.

Many old master etchings besides those of Rembrandt are available in the art market, and they are quite popular among collectors. You should always feel confident that etchings and other graphic works are not unknown or unverifiable entities. Indeed, they have for years been collected by kings and queens, the rich and the poor. Libraries abound in records of their execution and ownership; only a small percentage of such records can be mentioned here.

BOOKS ON OLD MASTER GRAPHICS

An excellent and complete series of source books containing more than eight thousand of the most important graphic works in the German school from the fifteenth to the eighteenth centuries is F. W. H. Hollstein's *German Engravings, Etchings and Woodcuts ca. 1400-1700.* The same scholar has also prepared a compilation of some seventeen thousand prints of the Dutch and Flemish schools; it is entitled *Dutch and Flemish Etchings, 1450-1700.* Wherever known, the states are recorded.

NINETEENTH CENTURY FRENCH GRAPHICS

Loys Delteil, one of the greatest French art historians, has prepared a magnificent thirty-one volume, completely illustrated set, recording the works of the major nineteenth and twentieth century French engravers and etchers. The books are entitled *Le Peintre-Graveur Illustré, XIX et XX Siecles.* You will find this series accurate and meticulous. Delteil catalogues the recorded works of Millet, Ingres, Delacroix, Corot, Degas, Toulouse-Lautrec, Zorn, Rodin, Daubigny, and Goya, to name only a few, and systematically arranges them for easy checking of measurements, edition sizes, and descriptions of states. Also in this series is a special ten-volume compilation of all of Daumier's recorded lithographs. Daumier, one of the most prolific artists of all time, created more than 4,400 original lithographs. You should be aware that a great many of his lithographs were printed on the reverse sides of newsprint paper. Today these are worth far less than those done on heavier French paper, and are usually valued at no more than five dollars to fifteen dollars. If, then, you want to collect fine Daumier caricatures and political cartoons, we advise you to seek the lithographs done on the heavier paper—the ones that are of the best quality, and unique in their freshness.

ENGLISH ETCHING AND ENGRAVING

Charles Russel's *English Mezzotints and Their States,* spanning the two centuries between the first English mezzotints and those of the early nineteenth century, is an exceptional and enlightening source. If, within the field of English engraving, the popular subjects of William Hogarth are especially appealing to you, you can further explore his work in Arthur Mayger Hind's definitive *William Hogarth—His Original Engravings and Etchings.* The Hogarths on the market today are very tricky. They include, first, the original engraved work of Hogarth, all of which was edited in 1795-1797 by William Boydel in collaboration with the artist, and second, engravings done after the originals by Hogarth. The latter were drawn and engraved by Thomas Cooke in 1812 and 1820 and are usually signed with his printed signature in the lower right-hand corner. They are somewhat less valuable than those actually executed by Hogarth during his lifetime, but nonetheless desirable to own.

PIRANESI

Piranesi's most popular and dramatic architectural engravings are called *The Prison Series,* or *Carcieri,* and the *Views of Rome,* or

Veduta Da Roma. In Hind's catalogue of these two series you will find a complete list of Piranesi's published works, reproductions of the series, and descriptive listings of each of the individual views.

Original Piranesi etchings were first executed by Giambattista Piranesi (1720-1778) with his sons Francesco and Pietro and his daughter Laura also working on their father's plates. The early states, printed in the mid-1700's in both Rome and Paris, are the most valuable Piranesi etchings. Later editions of the Piranesis' work were printed by the Italian government and have been sold for many years as souvenirs. They were printed as far into the twentieth century as the plates would allow, until the impressions were of such poor quality that most of the detail was lost. The etchings in the later editions bear the stamp of the Regia Calcografia in Rome; this stamp is located in the tip of the lower right-hand corner of the etching. Be sure you examine the detail of all Piranesi etchings. If your dealer represents a work to you as an early edition, make sure he stipulates this in writing. If you collect Piranesi architectural renderings you should not confuse the photographic reproductions with original work. A good Piranesi etching in an early state of the *Views of Rome* should cost about ninety dollars or more unframed, according to subject matter. The etching of the *Colosseum* will, for instance, be more valuable than that of the *Pyramid of Caius Cestius.* The later inexpensive Piranesis made by the government for the souvenir trade sell for a maximum of twenty-five dollars to thirty dollars and are not nearly so important or well delineated as the earlier renderings.

JAPANESE PRINTS

The standard reference for Japanese color woodcuts is Sir Lawrence Binyon's *Japanese Colour Prints.* This book illustrates many of the major seals and trademarks of the key artists, and, in many instances, the original woodcuts, whether genre, landscapes, flowers, actors, or birds.

The appealing and vivid Japanese woodcuts were first collected by artists in Europe during the late 1850's, and were originally appreciated for their formal geometric patterns and spatial arrangements. At the same time the introduction of aniline dyes enabled the master craftsmen like Hiroshige, Hokusai, and their followers to make their woodcuts especially brilliant and colorful.

Contemporary collectors are especially fond of the eighteenth and nineteenth century woodcuts. Also on the market, however, are woodcuts of lesser value printed early in the twentieth century for use in illustrated books; in fact, these are still being printed today. You can now buy a Japanese print executed in the twentieth century for from five dollars to ten dollars, which is a great contrast to the rare, high caliber nineteenth century print costing from sixty dollars to hundreds of dollars, depending upon the artist and subject matter. The best woodcut prints of the old Japanese are those done prior to the twentieth century for, as the wood block is used repeatedly, colors fade and the composition can become generally blurred. You can find late twentieth century examples having printed color so poorly applied that it runs beyond the boundary of the printed line.

COLLECTORS' MARKS

One of the most interesting aspects of collecting and verifying original art is the study of collectors' marks, or collectors' stamps as they are more popularly called. These, significant to both the historian and the collector, are usually found either in the margins or on the reverse sides of etchings, drawings, engravings, and other works. They usually appear as stamped initials, signatures, crests, coats of arms, names, letters, geometric patterns, intertwined forms, numbers, Oriental marks, crosses, and other similar objects. Many public and private collections including those of museums and of artists use these marks. You should look for them, as well as for gallery and exhibition labels, which are some-

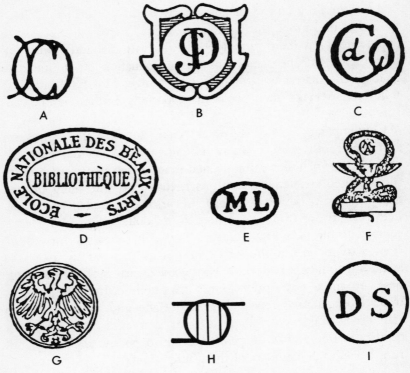

Some collectors' marks: (a) Charles Daubigny, French painter and engraver; (b) Charles Jourdeuil, French painter and collector; (c) H. A. Cornill-d'Orville, director of the Stadel Museum, Frankfort; (d) Ecole des Beaux-Arts, Paris; (e) the Louvre Museum; (f) Dr. Max A. Goldstein, American collector; (g) The German National Museum, Nuremberg; (h) Amand-Durand, French editor and publisher;

times affixed to the back of a picture and are similar in nature to collectors' stamps.

Collectors' stamps are in their way diaries for a particular work of art, for they identify the ownership of a work from the time it leaves the artist's hand until the present. You should understand, however, that only a limited number of the prints and drawings

(i) D. Schindler, seventeenth century Swiss collector; (j) Eugene Delacroix; (k) Musée Boymans, Rotterdam; (l) Edgar Degas; (m) Museum of Fine Arts, Boston; (n) Library of Congress, Washington; (o) Victoria and Albert Museum, London; (p) W. J. White, English engraver; (q) Bibliotheque Nationale, Paris; (r) Sir Joshua Reynolds.

found in the market today bear such marks. This is because only a limited number of famous collectors used them, and it in no way means that an etching or drawing lacking such a mark is necessarily of inferior quality. Rather, you should consider that collectors' marks, when and if they do appear, are usually good signs and excellent guarantees of high quality.

Because collectors' stamps cannot always be interpreted upon initial inspection, Frits Lugt's *Les Marques de Collections* is an extremely helpful reference. It contains photographic reproductions of all the known famous collectors' stamps, the colors in which they appear, and concise paragraphs about the collectors. Some of the most popular collectors' stamps are reproduced here.

LIMITED AND UNLIMITED EDITIONS

Etchings, woodcuts, engravings, lithographs, and other graphic forms are all artist originals, and are the artist's method of creating more than one example of a given work of art. In the contemporary art market these originals, etchings, lithographs, or whatever, appear either in limited or in unlimited editions. If they are unlimited editions, you cannot tell how many examples of the given print were produced before the plate was destroyed, if it was destroyed at all. With limited editions, however, the artist tells you the set number of prints he has pulled or printed.

NUMBERED EDITIONS

Contemporary limited editions are usually numbered in the lower left-hand corner in the order of their pull. They vary in size from editions of five prints to as many as four hundred prints, and perhaps even more. If an etching is numbered 4/50, this means that the edition to which it belongs is limited to fifty examples, and this particular one is the fourth made by the artist. While these fifty are similar works, each is different in its effects of color tone, line heaviness, and over-all feeling. *Catalogues raisonnés* never elaborate on the differences between the prints of various individual numbers, but they do describe edition sizes and the types of paper on which the works can be found. If, then, a dealer represents a Picasso poster (to choose but one possible example) as belonging to a limited edition, you should do some research of your own in Vollard's *Picasso Lithographie*. You may discover that this particular poster was printed in unlimited numbers. If so, it may be worth far less than the dealer's asking price. While it is extremely rare that a dealer would misrepresent an edition size, you should nevertheless know these fine points of verification.

You might wonder about the value of print number 49/50 as compared to that of print number 1/50. Prints of high and low numbers are equally valuable, and, in many instances the print with the higher number can be superior in quality and texture to a print of a lower number. The number of a print, then, should never be the deciding factor in making a purchase. Besides, considering the fact that an edition undoubtedly has world-wide distribution, each example is even more significant than the size of the edition might at first imply.

The numbering of limited editions did not begin until the 1920's. Before this, artists usually recorded in their own personal files and records the number of examples they issued from their etched plates or lithograph stones. In many instances they also noted this information on their etchings. Joseph Pennell, the celebrated early twentieth-century American etcher, often wrote the size of the edition on each of his etchings, but not the individual pull number of that particular example.

ARTIST PROOFS

Before an artist makes an edition, whether limited or unlimited, he first pulls trial proofs. In many instances these trial proofs, or artist proofs as they are called today, were the first states of the old-master etchings. Just as the numbering of an edition is penciled on the finished etching, artist proofs are similarly labeled "artist proof" or, if French, *Epreuve d'Artiste* (often abbreviated E.A.). There are many collectors who specialize in collecting artist proofs, for they are in many instances the preliminary studies of the finished product.

CANCELLED PLATES

Before the development of steel-faced plates in the twentieth century, the metal plates from which large editions were pulled could begin to show signs of wear by the time the printing was com-

Edgar Degas, French. *Ballet Dancer*
(etching from a cancelled plate).

pleted. Unfortunately, however, these plates have sometimes been
used for printing long after the death of an artist, and not according to his wishes. The resulting examples are often blurred, and
the lines discontinuous, but your familiarity with the graphic
media should help you immediately identify the marks of a worn
plate. Moreover, many artists now cancel their plates at the com-
pletion of an edition by boring holes in them or marking the
faces. Frederick Keppel, Jean François Millet's American dealer,
cancelled many of Millet's plates by boring holes in them. Edgar
Degas simply drew a large "X" over the face of his. As a discerning buyer you should always avoid impressions of inferior quality
and those bearing indications of the cancelled plate.

Berthe Morisot, French. *Swans* (etching from a cancelled plate).
Notice bored holes at left and right.

RESTRIKES

Goya's social and political commentaries in *Los Caprichos, Los
Proverbios,* and the *Disasters of War* are all very much in demand
in today's art market. As with Piranesis, an even and continuous
quality is important to observe in the bitten line of a Goya etching. Only the first two or three states, printed early in the nineteenth century, have this quality. A fine early state of one of
Goya's *Disasters of War* should bring approximately one hundred
twenty-five dollars. You should know, however, that as recently
as 1931, the Spanish government, owning Goya's original etched
plates, printed from them, making what are called government
restrikes. Do not confuse these less valuable examples with the

earlier and more valuable editions. On the most recent restrikes the lines are not clearly defined and sometimes not continuous because the etched plate was worn. The detail is dark and muddied, and generally the prints are worth from $10 to $20 each. Compare these two phases of Goya's etchings, the rarer and more highly sought after 1797 edition and the 1931 government restrike.

THE SIGNATURE

People often wonder whether or not a work of art is more valuable or better authenticated when it is signed. Though authentic old-master etchings are often unsigned, the art-collecting public still seems to consider the signature an important criterion for purchasing oils, watercolors, lithographs, etchings, drawings, and all forms of art. Of course, the signature is never an automatic sign that a work of art is genuine. In fact, for graphics in particular, signing the finished product was not a practice until the last century. There are two ways a graphic work can be signed: first, the artist may sign the plate or stone; second, he may sign each print—usually in the lower right-hand margin—after the edition is pulled. The concept of the signature has become important partly because of snob appeal and partly because of the artist's desire to distinguish his own works from those done by mechanical-reproduction processes. Whistler signed some of his works, others he did not. When he signed them individually in pen or pencil, he usually placed his famous butterfly signature somewhere within the margin of the print. At other times he signed only within the plate. Rembrandt and Goya never signed their works in pencil, but only in the plate. The great nineteenth century French masters like Millet and Pissarro hardly ever signed their etchings in pencil, and some of their rarest and most valued works are those left unsigned.

Today, artists take great pride in signing works of art. Most of the contemporary works in limited editions are signed by the artist in pen or pencil in the lower right-hand margin. Picasso often signs his work in red pencil. Dali considers each signature an individual masterpiece, a further expansion of the artist and his desire to create something beautiful. Each work is unique not only because of the color tonalities and the definition of line, but also because it is signed with a different "Dali." Once we saw him so concerned about the importance of his signature that he signed the same color lithograph three times.

The signatures of artists with permanent representation in a single gallery throughout their careers are usually well known by their dealers. For instance, James Graham and Sons in New York handles the Everett Shinn estate. This gallery is quite familiar with the artist's work and can authenticate any Shinn drawing or study brought to their attention. Likewise, any gallery that handles an artist's work exclusively is a good source of verification.

ESTATE SIGNATURES

A signature that looks printed or stamped is probably an estate signature and should not be confused with a collector's stamp. Estate signatures are placed on the artist's unsigned works by the executors of his estate. Upon his death these signatures label everything within the artist's collection as authentic. The unsigned works of Derain, Davies, Léger, and Maillol bear studio or estate stamps that in no way depreciate their value. Very often, in place of the estate stamp, the artist's wife or the executor himself will sign a finished product. Reginald Marsh's widow signed a great many of her husband's unsigned works and placed her initials P. M. (Peggy Marsh) after the signature.

HONORARY SOCIETIES

There are many artists who belong to famous societies and add to their signatures the initials of the society to which they belong. The famous National Academy of Design is one of the most distinguished societies of artists. The renowned nineteenth

century American landscape artist Bruce Crane usually signed his
oils Bruce Crane, N.A., the abbreviation for the National Academy. The contemporary American Watercolor Society members
usually follow their signatures with the initials A.W.S. To belong
to such a society is an honor and an indication that the artist has
received considerable recognition. Because he has earned his
membership within this select society, he tells you of his creden-
tials by signing his name and following it with the initials to which
he is entitled. Popular English watercolors of the nineteenth century are often signed with the name of the artist and the initials
R.W.S., which refer to the Royal Watercolor Society, the select
English group.

A CODE OF ETHICS: THE PRINT COUNCIL OF AMERICA

The more the collector learns about art, the more he protects
himself against a possible purchase of the fraudulent. But the
galleries protect him, too. Many subscribe to a code of ethics
recently set forth by the Print Council of America, a nonprofit
organization that dedicates itself to the appreciation of fine original prints. Their much-needed code is the first designed to
safeguard both the dealer and the collector. Those who join the
council pledge to subscribe to the code's standards, which are of the
highest order. Membership now totals nearly two hundred qualified, reputable print dealers, a directory of whom is available from
the Print Council of America, 527 Madison Avenue, New York,
New York 10017.

The standards set by the council were formulated with the advice and assistance of important collectors, museum curators, and
recognized dealers throughout the country. The subscribing
dealer receives a certificate confirming that he has vowed to provide, to the best of his ability and knowledge, all available information about every print he offers. This certificate is generally
situated in a prominent spot in the gallery. In time, more and
more dealers will be displaying it, for the code is a clear indica-

tion of decided progress in the field of graphic art.

The council defines an original print as a work of art in which

The artist himself has created the master image in or upon the plate, stone, woodblock or other material for the purpose of creating the print. The impression is made directly from the said material by the artist or pursuant to his directions. . . . The finished print is approved by the artist.

The Print Council's definition of an original print makes no mention of the artist's signature. Today, however, most original prints made in limited editions are usually signed by the artist.

With the definition of an original as a basis, the dealer standards published by the Print Council state:

1. A dealer should not describe any print as an original print, original etching, original lithograph, original engraving, original woodcut or the like, unless it *is* an original print as defined . . . above.

2. A dealer should deliver to a buyer a written invoice for prints sold, distinguishing reproductions from original prints in all printed matter, including catalogues, advertisements, and upon all invoices.

3. Catalog descriptions of prints should include all pertinent and significant information available with respect to such matters as collaboration on plate, signature or numbering by others than the artist, processes used and who used them, condition of print (such as cut margin or restoration), states, size of edition and number of impression, signature, date of execution, date of impression, cancellation of plate. Such information shall be conveyed to the buyer and shall, upon request, be entered on the invoice.

4. Dealers should use their best efforts to obtain from artists, publishers, and other sources, and to make available to the public, evidence that work is original; a description of how each print was made; and other pertinent facts such as catalog information and number.

5. Dealers should help members of the public to understand the difference between a reproduction and an original print, explaining processes of printmaking and using their best efforts to foster knowledge

and appreciation of fine prints, new and old, avoiding unusual and misleading terms such as "heliograph" which conceal the fact that a reproduction is not an original print.

THE LEGAL ASPECT

People often wonder when or if a legal case can be made if they purchase a fraudulent work of art. Legally, art is a commodity to be traded in the market place. The rules are few and logical. The law is blind to the nature of the art. It sees only the commercial transaction—the contract, its making, and its consummation.

Buying art at *auctions* is at the buyer's risk. All reputable auction galleries state in the front of their catalogues that they are making no representations as to the authenticity of the art works offered for sale. This "no representation" language is repeated publicly by the auctioneer at the beginning of the sale. It indicates one of the conditions of the sale, and the bidder consequently has no cause for complaint if he afterward discovers that he has bought a fake. If, then, you are trying to locate a bargain at an auction, be as certain as you can about the authenticity of your purchase. It will be too late after the sale.

When buying from a reputable dealer, you are usually on safe ground. Although even a reputable dealer can unknowingly make mistakes, he does not make a "no representation" claim and must therefore either accept returns of purchases discovered to be fakes or appear in court if sued. Suppose, then, you buy an etching by Piranesi. The dealer claims it is an excellent buy. Later, however, one of your friends, a collector, looks at it and declares it a reproduction. Observation through a magnifying glass subsequently reveals that it is a photographic reproduction process. The next day you try to return the etching. A reputable dealer will accept the return, refund your purchase price, and even add an apology. But if you encounter a more stubborn or less honest dealer— which is always possible—you may have to sue to recover your money. Then, only if you convince the court that the picture was misrepresented, can you recover your purchase price. The best thing to do when making any purchase is to have the dealer state on the invoice, bill of sale, or receipt the exact description of the work, the artist's name, and the medium of the work. These papers, with other statements of ownership and exhibition, are important evidence of provenance, and are handy records for resale purposes. You should always save the papers and leave any gallery stamps or museum labels on frames or wherever they are. And if you have anything reframed, caution the framer to replace the stickers on the new frame.

As we have noted, transactions with dealers are different from those at auctions. At the auction it is "let the buyer beware," but with the dealer it is usually the opposite. You rely on the dealer's representations, and he must, in most cases, back them up. Sometimes, however, even the dealer is not sure of the authenticity of the art work; the reputable gallery man will then tell you so. This is especially true of unsigned pieces. Like the auctioneer, the dealer may say: "We think that this is a Corot, but we are not sure." The work may reflect the style, the stroke, or the subject matter of Corot, but no one is certain that he executed it. Under these circumstances it is up to you to decide whether you want it badly enough to buy it. But if you do, don't try to return it. You can't.

There have been law suits involving all sorts of fraudulent art—forgeries, copies, reproductions, and even replicas (when the artist has done the same painting twice, the experts must decide which is the original and which is the replica). What makes these cases very interesting is the violent disagreement among the experts about authenticity. Naturally, if the artist is living, these questions are seldom an issue.

One of the most sensational cases involving authenticity was brought against the legendary early twentieth century art dealer Sir Joseph Duveen, who collected for such famous entrepreneurs as J. P. Morgan and the Ford family. This litigation involved *La*

Belle Ferronnière, a painting by Leonardo da Vinci, whose owner offered the canvas for sale. Duveen, in a statement published in a New York newspaper, declared the work a copy. After this condemnation, the painting became unsalable. Duveen was promptly sued for damages by the owner. The experts—and there were many—could not reach a conclusive decision as to the da Vinci's authenticity, even with the use of specialized X-ray techniques, which are often employed by museums to examine the pigment and canvases of old oil paintings. The jury could not arrive at a decision either. Before a retrial could be held, however, the case was settled out of court, with Duveen finally paying a large sum for damages to the owner of the painting.

Though most of the original art in the market today *is* authentic, the collector certainly owes it to himself to be as well informed about verification as possible. Verification is just another aspect of art collecting that can be easily learned and greatly enjoyed. In a short time you can develop the ability to determine the authenticity of almost any work of art presented to you. From the numerous specialized reference texts available in libraries, in which originals may be recorded, to the knowledge you acquire by observation and familiarity with original media, you will learn that it can be easy to authenticate many original works of art. This is triply valuable because it can lead to any one of three possible conclusions—that the work is inferior to what is represented and therefore *not really* worth the price; that it is the same as represented and *probably* worth the price; or—the epitome of art collecting—superior to what is represented and *worth more than* the price asked.

Terms and Abbreviations
Which Appear Again and Again on Old Prints

SYMBOL	DENOTES
Ad vivum	that a portrait was done "from life" and not after a painting
Aq., aquaf., aquafortis	the name of the etcher
D., del., delin., delineavit	the name of the draftsman
Des., desig.	the name of the designer
Direx., Direxit	work under direction by a certain master
Ex., exc., excu., excud., excudit, excudebat	the name of the publisher
F., fe., f^t, fec., fec^t, fecit, fa., fac., fac^t, faciebat	by whom the engraving was executed
Imp.	the printer's name
Inc., inci., incid., incidit, incidebat	who "incised" or engraved the plate
Inv., invenit, inventor	the designer or inventor of a picture
Lith. de	in whose establishment a lithograph was printed and who printed it
P., pictor, pingebat, pinx, pinx^t, pinxit	who painted the picture from which the engraving was made
S., sc., scul., sculp., sculpsit, sculpebat, sculptor	the name of the engraver; appears after his name

4   *Where to Buy*

Honoré Daumier, lithograph.

Successful art collecting invariably depends upon where and how treasures are bought. Whether you are relying upon sheer instinct, impulse, or a highly sophisticated knowledge and taste, there are literally hundreds of sources you can tap to begin or continue collecting. At the present time there are more than one thousand art galleries in the United States. Their largest concentration is in New York City; in fact, almost one-half of all the galleries in America can be found between 57th and 86th streets running from Madison Avenue to Third Avenue, or just outside these boundaries. Interspersed among them are several universally renowned museums of art—the Metropolitan, the Whitney Museum, the Museum of Modern Art, the Frick Collection, the Jewish Museum, the Guggenheim Museum, and the Gallery of Modern Art. Rarely, however, will a work of art appear for public sale once it has been purchased by or contributed to a museum.

THE ART GALLERY

On a typical Saturday afternoon in New York, art lovers spend time in both the galleries and museums. Most gallery visiting and most buying occur between mid-September and late May, the time known in the art market as the art season. In fact, many galleries close during the summer to vacation and to restock their inventories with foreign and domestic works. Do not assume, however, that all of them close; many galleries are both ready and anxious to do business during the warm summer months. Moreover, this can often be to your advantage, for you can wander through galleries browsing in solitude and leisure, since patronage greatly decreases during the summer. Also, you can often buy for strikingly low prices. Some of the best bargains ever available in the market emerge during the summer, simply because the galleries open all year round must offer attractive prices to make enough sales to offset their overhead costs. It is likely that as the demand for art continues to increase, more and more art galleries will remain active during the summer.

While New York's Madison Avenue is one of the leading art capitals of the world, there are growing centers elsewhere. Ranking among these are Chicago, Los Angeles, Philadelphia, San Francisco, Cleveland, Washington, Dallas, Boston, and Atlanta, all of whose art markets have mushroomed during the past ten years. It used to be that one had to journey to New York or Europe for art purchases. Now there are many scattered sources, and even some new methods of distribution, the most recent being department stores that are now making high quality, original works of art available to the public in areas where until recently people had to travel hundreds of miles even to see, much less to buy, original works of art.

The art market is unique in many respects. One of them is the strange, phenomenal speed with which dealers and traders, regardless of location, know when pictures are sold. A famous dealer once quipped: "If you were to sneeze in New York's art market, someone in California would say 'God bless you!' " Similarly, dealers who have good reputations are known among their colleagues and even among collectors, all of whom can offer you the benefit of their experience and opinions. But the best way of familiarizing yourself with art galleries and their offerings is to spend time visiting and revisiting those that appeal to you. Try to become acquainted with some of the reputable art dealers, the ones that seem to be respected by other art sellers and by collectors. Reputable and knowledgeable gallery owners can be invaluable sources not only of art but also of information, advice, and general assistance.

Some dealers stock what is referred to as "a general varied inventory"—that is, varieties of artists, subject matter, media, and periods of art. Others stock only a select and limited number of individual artists, commonly called "a stable of artists," whom they sponsor and feature exclusively. If you are looking for the work of a certain artist, inquire at the gallery in whose stable he belongs. Here you will probably find a great variety of examples to view, since the artist is represented exclusively by this dealer except, of course, for works that have been bought from the dealer's stable in the past and resold by the second owner to still another dealer. Some galleries combine both types of inventories, offering a general selection but also featuring special artists in their stable. Some galleries are known for their specialization in particular periods; others, in specific media. The Childs Gallery and the Vose Gallery, both in Boston, are, for instance, fine sources for nineteenth and twentieth century American art by well and lesser known painters; so are the Graham Gallery and the Sloan Gallery, both in New York. Also in New York is the unique and interesting Drawing Shop. Here you can find drawings of all periods of the most educated taste, and very often within the means of the beginning collector.

If you have never frequented art galleries before, you should start by visiting as many as possible. Some will have a greater appeal to your taste and pocketbook than others. The more time you spend, the more familiar you can become with the different types of galleries, the artists they usually feature, and what schools of art can best be purchased at what source. For the most part, art galleries are accommodating, eager to answer your questions, and, even more important, reputable and honest. Yet, sometimes those who have never been inside art galleries say that these establishments are so snobbish and ultraelegant that the minute you step inside you feel you must approach the exhibit on tiptoe and make comments only in low whispers. This common misconception should be dispelled at once—and it can be— merely by entering a gallery. Even if it is the first you have ever visited, and even if you are only browsing, go with confidence. Art galleries welcome all who are interested. If they are to maintain their business they need customers, and one of these customers may be you!

BUYING AT AUCTION

Another of the many sources available for buying fine art is the public auction. This business has existed for centuries, but during the past decade its rate of growth and acceptance has accelerated incredibly. It used to be that buying at auctions was limited to the aristocratic connoisseur. Today, however, it is viewed as the "thing to do"; some of the more important sales even become congenial social events. The public auction is, then, just what its name implies—it is public, and all are invited to partake in the competition and bidding. Newspapers and many periodicals carry regular listings of exhibitions and sales; you should attend any that sound interesting to you.

A private owner, a dealer, or an estate that liquidates a given

A Rembrandt painting—*Aristotle Contemplating the Bust of Homer*—being sold at public auction at Parke-Bernet Galleries, New York. Mr. Louis J. Marion, the auctioneer in this sale, is shown on the rostrum. Courtesy of the Parke-Bernet Galleries, Inc., New York.

art work or collection of art at auction is charged a commission
for these services by the auction house. The commissions to the
auction gallery are generally lower in Europe—10 to 15 per cent
of the price eventually received. In the United States they usually
vary from 15 to 22 per cent of the price. All good auction houses
prepare catalogues for each of their sales. These give information
about each picture, its artist, title, medium, size, subject matter,
general appearance, and former owners. Catologues are usually
available prior to the actual auction; they are immensely important
for you to consult because buying at auction is at your own risk.
As previously mentioned, there is no such thing as a return at a
public auction. You are advised to read the terms of sale which
you find at the beginning of all auction catalogues; study their
specific objectives and conditions, especially concerning authenticity, provenance, and history of ownership or place of origin.
There you will learn that an auction house functions merely as a
middleman, a liquidating and selling agent.

Some auction houses go to greater lengths than others to research the authenticity of art works they accept and offer. The
key difference between the great auction galleries and those of
lesser stature often rests with their art experts. For this reason, the
well-known Parke-Bernet Galleries in New York City, and both
Sotheby's and Christie's in London, as well as the Palais Galiera in
Paris have made every effort to hire experienced professionals
who screen and verify the authenticity of all works of fine
art offered to them for public sale. You should not ignore this fact
when deciding whether or not to purchase original art at a public
auction. Although a work is not always guaranteed to be authentic just because it comes from a public or well-known collection, a
work whose prior ownership is noted usually sells more quickly
than one that is anonymously auctioned.

Once you have received and studied an auction catalogue, you
should visit the exhibition of the works listed in it. These exhibitions precede a sale for a specified amount of time, perhaps three

to five days, and are for your inspection. You can even bring to them any expert whom you might want to have appraise your contemplated purchase. At the same time, you can also obtain the gallery's estimates of anticipated prices for the actual auction sale. You should record these in your catalogue next to each corresponding item. When the final bids are made, you can, by comparison, determine whether the gallery estimates were generally high or low, and what has been the general trend of the prices. When you receive an estimate at an exhibition, you should already have some idea of the actual market price on an equivalent work; that is, what it would cost were you to buy something like it from a gallery. As a general rule, auction prices are about 80 per cent of the market prices on similar items, but do not include the same assurances and guarantees.

Save the catalogue in which you have noted the actual prices bid at an auction. It is your best guide for the next sale you will attend. We shall mention again and again in this book that there is no such thing as a bargain with a work of art. Artists have established market prices. The same is true at auction. If a price diverges considerably from the norm, one of two things is probably indicated—that there are no takers for this specific work because of its subject matter, color, or style, or because the authenticity is questionable. Otherwise, prices are generally quite consistent.

Never buy a work of art at auction unless you have first examined it carefully at the exhibition prior to the sale. Works of art may look magnificent under flood lights, but you might well be disappointed after the auction if you should buy an item you have not examined before. Under these lights flaws such as minor tears, stains, and peeling are sometimes invisible from a distance. As the auction catalogue cautions in the language of the old legal maxim, "Let the buyer beware."

Buying art at public sale is always by bids accepted by the auctioneer from the audience. Even Rembrandt's legendary *Aris-*

Exhibition of graphics prior to a sale. Courtesy of the Parke-Bernet
Galleries, Inc., New York.

totle Contemplating the Bust of Homer was sold this way. In
1962, this painting brought the highest price ever paid (up to that
time) at auction for an original work of fine art—$2,300,000.
The auctioneer begins by suggesting an opening bid, which someone in the gallery usually meets. Try not to be the opening bidder.
The most successful buyers at an auction are those who watch the
succession of bids and the number of dollars by which they increase. You can enter the competition at any time, merely by
raising your hand toward the auctioneer, though seasoned bidders
may employ such curious techniques as a wink, a nod, or even a
twitch. Some people wait a long time before declaring a bid, even
as late as the auctioneer's final warning, which is usually his last

The "fair warning" stage in auctioning Fragonard's *La Liseuse.*
Courtesy of Parke-Bernet Galleries, Inc., New York.

hesitation before bringing down the hammer and declaring
"Sold!"

Bids can increase by five, ten, twenty-five, fifty, or hundred-
dollar stages, and in the case of more expensive pictures, in mul-
tiples of thousands. Sometimes they increase steadily for a while,
but toward the end, as the auctioneer tries to reach a peak price,
they can be cut in half. Take, for example, a picture estimated to
bring eighty dollars. Starting with an opening bid of thirty dollars,
the auctioneer goes on to accept bids in increments of ten. He
reaches only seventy dollars, hears no further offer, and then says
"Fair Warning." At this moment you are perfectly within your
rights to bid "Seventy-five." But in most instances such bidding is

subject to the veto of the auctioneer. He may or may not accept your bid, but you should always risk a try! If it is accepted you are known in official terms as the successful bidder, and the person who bid prior to you is the underbidder.

Sometimes at public auction pictures are offered in "lots." This means that a group of items is sold for one inclusive price. On some occasion you might want only one or several parts of a lot. You must then decide the value of the few items you want to own in comparison with the cost of the whole lot, which is never broken up.

BUYING FROM THE DEPARTMENT STORE

Three years ago an entirely new concept of art selling and merchandising emerged in the American market. At that time, Sears, Roebuck and Co. began collecting original fine art for sale in its retail stores. Under the direction of art authority Vincent Price, Sears has been able to circulate its collection throughout the United States, Canada, and Mexico, always for sale and always framed. Other similar merchandising companies have begun to follow Sears' example, and their art exhibitions and sales have aided both the amateur and professional collector. Though in some areas of the country fine art has never even been available, and in other areas has never been available at competitive prices, people in all sections of the country can now choose from among many such local department stores. Many, such as Sears, offer credit arrangements, and some have even become members of the Print Council of America's Code of Ethics Standards Committee. Buying original art can be just as easy as buying practically any other basic home furnishing. A good department store has a varied collection—from the old masters to the contemporaries—and offers work in all media. In this way both the amateur and the established collector can select works of art from a myriad of possibilities, and all in one place.

BUYING FROM A CATALOGUE

Another vehicle currently available to the art collector, and a recent innovation in art buying, is the catalogue. Some of the best buys in the art market today come to the collector via this avenue. Most catalogues are prepared semiannually, and present excellent opportunities to purchase recent etchings, lithographs, engravings, woodcuts, and other media by both "name" and "up-and-coming" artists. In many instances purchasing in this manner means saving a few dollars, since no costly display or high overhead charges are figured into the final price, and the saving is passed on to the customer. Sears, Roebuck and Company, The Print Council of America, and the Kennedy Galleries are pioneers in offering fine art from a catalogue. All of these organizations and others, recognizing the need for personal investigation and contemplation of an art purchase, provide some arrangements for home approval.

LOCAL EXHIBITIONS

You can sometimes buy art at benefit exhibitions and sales sponsored by local charities or religious institutions. Many such shows offer an unusually and perhaps unexpectedly wide variety of artists and media. Similar sales occur during the summer months in resort communities. While they usually concentrate on the work of regional artists, their offerings can be exceptionally stimulating and diversified.

ANTIQUE SHOPS

The antique shop has long been a mecca for the collector hoping to make a "find." While there certainly have been cases of lucky discoveries, the statement that this usually does not occur is more accurate than its opposite. Since antique shops receive a sizeable proportion of their wares from old estates, they frequently have art treasures in their inventories that have been in private collections for generations. Antique stores are, then, among the best sources for art work that dates back to the nineteenth century and earlier.

Antique stores can be found in all cities and on country roads. You should never hesitate to visit them and browse, even if merely to inform yourself about selections and costs. And remember that there is no such thing as a secondhand work of art. As long as it is accurately authenticated and reasonably priced, a purchase at any antique shop, and even in a thrift or junk shop, can be on a par with any you can make anywhere else. Don't forget, however, to include any costs you might have to incur for cleaning or restoring a picture. "Antiques" often bear the marks of old age. Professional repairs and cleaning can become expensive, so always keep this thought and the potential cost in mind.

BUYING DIRECTLY FROM THE ARTIST

Frequently an artist himself will sell his art to you. Although most established contemporaries have exclusive contracts with dealers who represent them, and sell their work only through their dealers, many artists represent themselves, and will sell their art directly. Buying this way does limit you to selecting from a single artist's work; try, therefore, to buy from those artists who have had formal training and at least some exhibition experience, and who are perhaps represented in some well-known collections. When you are purchasing directly from an artist, you should try to buy from one about whose background and predicted future you can gather some amount of knowledge—and, of course, from one whose work you like.

THE COMMISSION

Sometimes you can commission an artist. This means that for a given sum he will execute a work in a medium and on a subject that are agreeable to both of you. While most artists prefer not to be commissioned by individuals, there are many portrait artists whose entire livelihood comes from private commissions. Portraits, Inc. in New York, one of the leading art galleries specializing in portraits, has in its stable some of America's leading portrait artists.

The term "commission" as used in the art world also refers to the sponsorship, often financial, of a single art project by a major private, governmental, religious, or national organization. During the sixteenth century, the Vatican commissioned Michelangelo to paint the now famous *Last Judgment* in the Sistine Chapel in Rome. Several years ago the state of Israel asked Chagall to create in glass his renowned *Jerusalem Windows,* and recently the French government requested the monumental painted composition by Chagall, now in the dome of the famous Opéra in Paris.

COMPARATIVE SHOPPING

As we suggested earlier, comparative shopping is a phase of art collecting that cannot be neglected by the serious art collector. As a successful buyer of art you should have a good idea of what you are getting and what similar items can be found elsewhere. There are certainly instances where a lithograph, for example, is offered by a number of sellers at an identical price, but there are also times when, for any number of reasons, one seller will offer the same print at a better price than anyone else. A conscientious comparative shopper visits many galleries, has a good idea of the characteristic subject matter, media, and sizes of an artist's work, and has some way of comparing one of his works to similar examples at different sources. It is true that the living contemporary European and American artists like Picasso, Moore, Marini, Buffet, Dubuffet, Soyer, Evergood, Dehn, and others do have established market prices, but there are still variations between dealers that a discerning collector discovers while comparative shopping. This difference may be a few dollars or quite a few; it is often worth the search. Comparative shopping also permits you to select the best possible quality of an artist's work currently available in your local art market. It can also mean better frame quality, since that extra money can be applied to a frame, which of course must ultimately be figured into the final cost of your purchase.

Recently, a Marc Chagall hand-colored etching from *The Fables of Fontaine* was offered by two different art galleries within the same city. One offered the etching for $165, the other for $185. An example from this same series was recently offered at a public auction, and in the excitement of bidding a young collector paid $220 for a print which could have been bought at a lower price in a gallery. Knowledge of comparative values would prevent such overpayment.

The theory of comparative shopping applies to a concentration of galleries within a city or other local geographic region. It also applies to comparisons between art centers. There are certain kinds of art that are common to certain areas, and prices vary accordingly. The works of Raphael Soyer are, for example, very well known in the New York art center. Because of the demand there for his watercolors and drawings, and because Soyer's supply is not unlimited, the prices are higher in this peak-demand area than in, for example, the Atlanta or Dallas market. Intracity comparative shopping teaches you to shop your own local market thoroughly and to know who is selling where and at what price. What is popular in one area may not be so popular in another. As a result, you may be able to make a better buy if you can shop both within a city and between cities.

HOME TRIALS AND APPROVALS

Art, like other commodities, can be taken home for your approval. The cardinal rule in collecting art is that you like what you select. You will be the one to live with it and consequently you must be completely satisfied. Many collectors who are first venturing into collecting need some provision for a trial of what is to them something new and untested; others want to determine as best they can whether a work will "stand the test of time." Most reputable art dealers provide and even encourage home approval, usually for pictures costing more than a hundred dollars. You can thus have a chance to live with your selection for a few days and discuss it with your family and friends. For expensive pictures, feel perfectly free to ask for such an opportunity—even the most established collectors like to enjoy a period of acquaintance before making any final decisions.

The concept of a home trial parallels a rental program presently being employed by some museums, such as the Museum of Modern Art in New York, the Baltimore Museum, the Albright Art Gallery in Buffalo, the Dayton Art Institute, the Cleveland Art Association, the Art Institute of Chicago, the San Francisco Museum, the Dallas Museum of Fine Arts, the Walker Art Center in Minneapolis, the Portland Art Museum in Portland, Oregon, the University of Miami, and by some art galleries. They will rent a work of art by the day, month, or year with an option to buy. In any case, you should never feel that it is impossible to live with a tentative choice before making a final decision.

PUBLICATIONS CONTAINING INFORMATION ON WHERE TO BUY

A number of different collectors' guides are currently being published. These offer you the opportunity to receive on a steady basis an up-to-date schedule of showings in all of the art markets, both domestic and foreign. Listings, classified by art center, provide the name of the art gallery, its address, the titles and dates of its current and near-future shows, and the names of its featured artists. This information is best presented in the following specialized periodicals, published monthly and available by subscription: *The New York Arts Calendar*, 369 Cathedral Station, New York, N.Y.; *The Art Gallery*, Ivoryton, Conn.; and *Pictures on Exhibit*, 30 East 60th Street, New York, N. Y.

If you would like to have additional gallery previews, you can follow those in your local Sunday newspaper art section, or read the listings and commentaries found weekly in such magazines as *Time* and *The New Yorker,* and monthly in *Art News* (4 East 53rd Street, New York, New York 10022) and *Arts Magazine* (41 East 57th Street, New York, New York 10022). Magazines and newspapers do editorialize, and they often review shows quite critically; don't necessarily avoid a show solely on the basis of a single unfavorable review.

5 Framing and Hanging

Honoré Daumier, lithograph.

HISTORICAL SIGNIFICANCE OF THE FRAME

The Egyptians began to surround their tomb monuments and religious artifacts with borders of gold as early as 1800 B.C. The Romans devised elaborate schemes of wall decoration in their villas and city dwellings from about 50 B.C. to 100 A.D. During the early-Gothic period in the twelfth century, artists placed molded wooden forms around panel paintings to make them fit into the architectural plans of chapels and churches. Yet only after paintings began to be treated as independently appealing entities rather than as mere church decorations were frames considered art works in themselves. Then, during the late-fifteenth century, specially trained craftsmen in Florence and Venice produced the earliest examples of picture frames specifically designed as aesthetic, self-expressive entities. Artisans soon followed suit throughout Italy, Spain, and Flanders. In France, too, the frame maker's craft came into its own, but on a more refined level, developing and maturing with the more graceful and elaborate beauty characteristic of the furniture and decorative art of that country.

One of the prime characteristics of the majority of "modern" frames is the absence of heavy traditional forms. The contemporary aesthetic focus is on the canvas, the edges of which are "finished" with thin moldings. The frame today has so dwindled that it draws immediate attention to the pure shape and size of the painting field, as well as to the images on it. This current taste or fashion perfectly illustrates the intimate relationship that the painting and its frame have had throughout the history of art. The effective frame always sensitively complements the painted field that it surrounds, and may relate to the painting in any number of ways. An ample selection of period and modern frames is available to the collector.

TASTEFUL FRAMING IS IMPORTANT

"Art is limitation, the essence of every picture is the frame." With these words Gilbert Keith Chesterton summarized his opinion about a frequently questioned relationship. Whether or not we agree with Chesterton, the fact remains that tasteful framing is essential to any pictorial image, and the *right* frame can indeed enhance an artist's expression. In a sense, the picture lives in its frame, and with it the viewer is led to the full enjoyment of the work. Georges Seurat, the French Post-Impressionist, considered an appropriate frame so important that he often *made his own,* using his characteristic pointillist technique for both picture and frame, and relating the colors of the two in a very complex way. *La Grande Jatte* in the Metropolitan Museum of Art in New York City well exemplifies Seurat's novel framing technique.

THE FRAME AS A COMPLEMENT TO THE PICTURE

The first and most important question to ask when you are selecting a frame is: "What am I framing?" The answer has to do with what frame makers call the spirit of a work of art. This spirit is often related to the school or era of the painting, and is especially essential to understand today, because period framing is one of the current trends. The basic principle of this technique is that the history of art is the best guide for frame selections. That is, to cite only two of numerous possible examples, paintings baroque in feeling require a baroque frame; similarly, paintings that are simple, linear, and contemporary in design require clean, unobtrusive, modern frames.

If blending or harmonizing frames with your works of art is less desirable to you than contrasting them, whether in spirit and feeling or in color and texture, then by all means contrast. A frame is improper only if it overpowers artistic expression, competes with a picture, distracts the viewer from the drawn image, or actively clashes with it. Guide yourself by the fact that, whether contrasted or matched with a work of art, a frame is acceptable and effective if it is not inordinately creative. A word of caution, too, about using color with your frame selection. People today are apt to pick out one color from the picture and repeat it throughout the frame. The result often is that the viewer cannot decide what to look at because the frame vies with the art work for his attention. Yet, cautions aside, you really cannot use any theory to tell whether a frame will be right for a given work of art until you come face to face with it. The most significant guide is the picture itself, for although there are traditional framing practices, there are certainly no set formulas. Some works of art seem to frame themselves, while others can be completed only by trial and error. One of the curious things about selecting frames is that the works of art you like the best often prove to be the hardest to frame.

THE FRAME AS DECOR

One of the most distressing trends in art today is the "decorator approach" to picture buying and framing. Just as there is nothing more tragic than buying an inferior work of art simply because it matches the rug or sofa pillows, there is nothing more absurd than misframing a fine work of art merely to match the coffee table. Visualize the *Mona Lisa* imprisoned in Danish modern and you will understand why you should never select frames merely to ornament a room. The first duty of the frame is to the picture. Its job is to enhance the picture by making it a pleasing focal point of the room, not to debase it by making the picture a mere wall decoration. The picture and its frame should stand on their own merits, or they do not deserve to be hung.

SELECTING YOUR FRAMER

There is a frame maker, or someone qualified to select frames with you, in practically every community in our country, but you will buy with double assurance if you have not only his opinions but also your own knowledge of proper and economical framing. Shop comparatively! At some stores you will find just a few of the standard frames, at others a larger and more varied selection. All shops differ, too, both in the quality and the price range of their offerings. Yet, regardless of all of these variables, one thing should be constant. The price quoted to you should always include these things: the molding; the matting; the glass (if it is needed); and the proper fitting of these components. As he figures the final frame price for you, the framer should list the cost of each of these individually.

As we mentioned earlier, you cannot really tally the final price of a work of art until you figure the cost of framing it properly and tastefully. Many galleries or auction houses sell unframed art; some offer mats; others include mats and frames. But either way, they should indicate, or you should make sure that you find out, exactly what each given price includes. And, if necessary, keep in mind the potential cost of framing. Today—to indicate what a difference such care on your part can make—there are two art sellers who offer *Annie Seated,* a small, delicate etching by the American master James Abbott McNeill Whistler. One asks forty dollars for the etching framed; the other, forty dollars unframed. With alert, knowledgeable shopping you can locate the former, and save many framing dollars!

A framer with a fine reputation is usually well known and recommended by his contemporary art dealers, who may them-selves frequent the firm they recommend. A good frame maker is one who is dependable, has the respect of his fellow art dealers, and is always cautious in the handling of your art work. He must see that the edges of a drawing or a print are never cut or trimmed, for this ultimately reduces their resale value. He should use a pure wheat paste or library paste on the hinges holding the work of art to the mat, never modern glues, which can eventually rot and discolor the paper. And he should never hinge all four corners of a print, for only if it hangs freely can it accommodate the shrinking or swelling of the mat on which it is mounted. He should also be careful to back the framed picture with good rag-content backboards, and not with wood-pulp backs. The latter, used many years ago, contain chemicals that can discolor the paper on which the art work is executed. Finally, look to see how well he has fitted and joined the corners of the frame. This is an excellent test for a competent framer.

An *exceptional* frame maker is also one who can offer you a variety of solutions to your particular framing problems, solutions in accord with your budget and your taste. See what the prices of all his frames are, his least as well as his most expensive. A work of art by any artist can be as eye-catching in a twenty-dollar frame as in one costing a hundred dollars. Don't be afraid to follow your own taste. While we caution against being overly creative, you are the person who will be living with the picture and frame. If they don't suit you it matters little what anyone else may say. In the final analysis you must follow the cardinal rule of collecting: buy what you like.

OBTAINING IDEAS FROM OTHERS

A trip to your favorite museum or art gallery is a good way to develop an eye for the best types of frames for different types of art. Museums change their exhibits almost every month, and new frames often accompany each exhibition. In addition to their own collections, museums sometimes display works of art lent to them by private collectors, who may buy more elaborate or costly frames, and whose selections offer additional possibilities for study. Before deciding on your own frames, try to determine why various selections were made, and ask yourself what other alternatives might have been desirable.

TYPES OF FRAMES

During the sixteenth century the Venetian master Titian designed and manufactured his own frames. Today few artists do so, but that is in one way at least an advantage, for history tells us that the prices of Titian's frames were as high as those of the compositions within them. Fortunately for our finances, then, frame making is today a very competitive business, and selections and prices are widely varied!

Frames are constructed on bases of wood, brass, aluminum, plastic, and synthetic woods. In fact, 75 per cent of those currently manufactured have some type of wood as their base, and are made in one of two ways—they are either hand carved or machine molded. The basic wooden frame is manufactured with a layer of gesso and, sometimes, a layer of red clay placed over the raw wooden stock. This clay acts as a protective layer to which

Hand carving a Spanish frame. Courtesy of Dain-Schiff Picture Framers, Inc., New York.

the final finish adheres, whether it is of gold, silver, metal leaf, paint, or any other substance.

There are innumerable types of frames on the contemporary market. Some are elaborate and antique in feeling; others are extremely linear in outline and of the modern tradition. One of the oldest, which frame makers faithfully reproduce today, is the Gothic or medieval frame. It is in the tabernacle rather than the four cornered style, shaped like the ornamental container used in a church for sacramental articles. It functions as an integral part of the work of art and perfectly complements icons, woodcuts, and similar works of the medieval period. Antique or Gothic

Hand finishing an Italian Renaissance frame. Courtesy of Dain-Schiff.

frames cannot be found in every frame shop, and are generally made specifically to order. Prices for them begin at about forty dollars for a frame 12 inches by 16 inches, including a board mat, glass, and fitting.* From there the prices increase according to the amount of labor and gold or other material required for the finish.

Italian Renaissance frames are more powerful than Gothic, heavier in feeling, often with very little decoration. They are sometimes painted with dark colors, and are especially well suited

---

* All subsequent frame prices are for 12 by 16 inch models, and all include board mat, glass, and fitting charges.

Applying gold leaf. Courtesy of Dain-Schiff.

Hand cutting a French mat. Courtesy of Dain-Schiff.

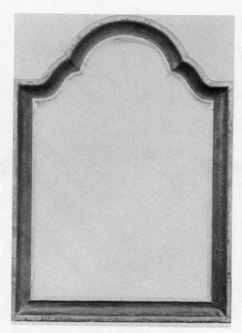

The Gothic frame. Courtesy of Dain-Schiff.

both to religious subjects and to the surrealistic compositions of such artists as Salvador Dali and Yves Tanguy. The price of this type of frame depends upon the amount of decoration and finish; it can range from fifteen to twenty-five dollars up to several hundred.

Closely related to the Italian Renaissance frame is the Spanish frame. Though its name might not imply as much, it, too, is a period frame, dating back to the late sixteenth century. Its rough surface has a strong, bold, chainlike appearance and is well matched with such twentieth century graphics as Picasso's early Expressionist and Cubist work, and examples by Rouault, Matisse, Chagall, Dali, and Braque. Because Spanish frames are

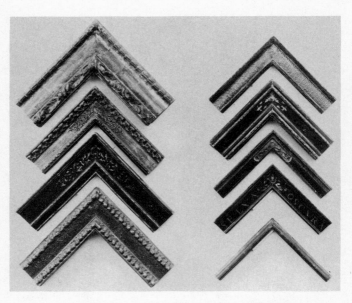

Italian Renaissance frames. Courtesy of Dain-Schiff.

hand carved, their prices can start at about forty-five to fifty dollars. But you can also find machine-reproduced examples which cost about half as much as the hand-carved versions. Do not hesitate to use such reproductions; many reputable collectors and museums find them, on the whole, to be very skillfully executed and aesthetically pleasing.

Unlike the highly elaborate Spanish frames, Dutch frames are plain and austere in appearance. They originated in northern Europe, where frame styles traditionally lack ornamental surface relief, and they are most successful with works enhanced by a simple statement: still lifes; such genre paintings as those by Jan Vermeer; the subjects of such "primitives" as the French Henri Rousseau and the American Grandma Moses; and also the work of the eighteenth- and nineteenth-century American artists in general.

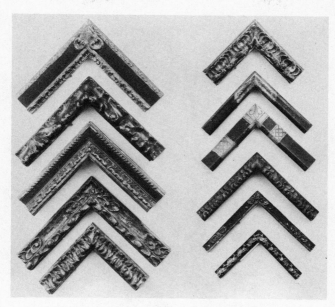

Spanish frames. Courtesy of Dain-Schiff.

Another group of popular frames are the French Louis XIII, XIV, XV, and XVI models. Louis XIII frames are straight panels, and usually have some sort of carved floral decoration somewhere within their design. Louis XIV frames have ornate corners that are delicately carved within the panels, often with scroll design. Louis XV and XVI frames have large corners, generally with extremely elaborate hand-carved sweeps, and little emphasis on decoration within the panels. These frames are probably the best solutions for modern paintings if you want something not only in good taste, but slightly more elaborate than the band or stripping frame. All of these French frames work well with examples of the Impressionist, Post-Impressionist, and Fauve schools of the late nineteenth and early twentieth century, including such well-known names as Pissarro, Renoir, Matisse, Signac, Dufy, Derain, and others. Louis XVI models are especially out-

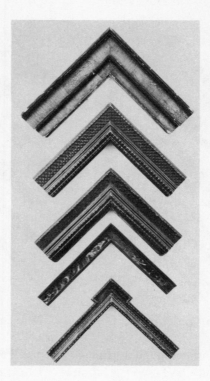

Dutch frames. Courtesy of Dain-
Schiff.

standing with American and English landscapes and scenes of the
nineteenth century. The French frames are, however, period
frames, and you may consequently have difficulty finding original
examples. But contemporary frame makers make artful facsimiles, usually priced at a minimum of thirty to forty dollars.

If your budget is limited and you would like a tasteful frame
for any medium of art, the popular and always successful modern
stripping or band frames are best. They are very clean, linear, and
undefined in pattern; they are also very moderately priced. Made
of wood, generally mahogany, their front edges are often painted

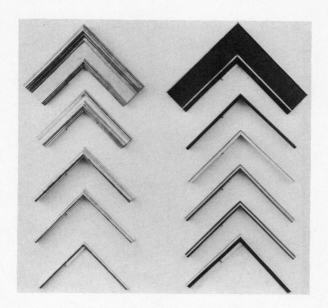

Modern frames. Courtesy of Dain-Schiff.

with gold trim or metallic silver. They go especially well with the
spirit of abstract pictures by such contemporaries as Jackson
Pollack, and with modern black and white, because they never
conflict with busy painted forms. They are also very complemen-
tary to modern geometrically conceived works, as, for example,
the mathematically proportioned Mondrian and Gris compositions, and are successful solutions for the works of Op artists like
Vasarely and Anuszkiewicz. Art galleries often use plain band or
stripping frames for hanging entire exhibitions, though sometimes
less expensive Tenite or plastic moldings are even more desirable.
These frames effectively enhance modern prints and drawings.
Like the band frames, they can be acquired for as little as twenty
to thirty dollars, and can range from there to forty or fifty. The
price depends upon the size and finish along the edges, which can
be gold, silver, or metallic Tenite.

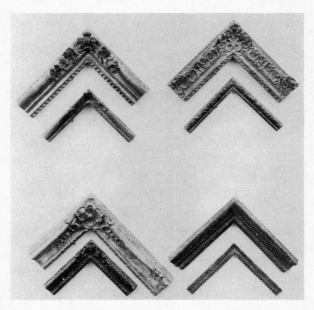

Design corners for French period frames: (*upper left*) Louis XIII; (*upper right*) Louis XIV; (*lower left*) Louis XV; (*lower right*) Louis XVI or Regency. Courtesy of Dain-Schiff.

A recent contemporary innovation is the shadow-spaced frame. This is usually a narrow wooden (stripped) frame with a space of approximately half an inch between the frame and the painting itself. Rather than enclosing the picture, it allows a breathing space for bold rhythms and rich colors, such as those found in many contemporary paintings.

GLASS

Glass is used in picture frames to protect works of art, especially drawings, watercolors, pastels, gouaches, and graphics. Several types are available, of which Grades A and B American Picture Glass are probably the best. They are of fine quality and, unlike others, do not discolor over a long period of time. Grade B is, of course, not as pure as Grade A, but both are more than satisfactory for picture framing. Unbreakable glasses are also readily available on the market, but they are generally very expensive. The best of these is thin Plexiglas, made of Lucite. It is generally twice the cost of Grades A and B American Picture Glass.

In recent years there has been a trend toward framing art works with nonreflective glass. Because this glass has an etched surface, it will refract light, and yield a nonglossy, varnished finish. Unfortunately, this effect can tend to dim and distort the true qualities of a work of art. In fact, in many instances it can make originals look like reproductions, which themselves are often framed with nonreflective glass. Moreover, since it requires that the work of art be flush with the glass, it is impossible to use for drawings and pastels, since the rubbing of the glass against the surfaces of these compositions would destroy them. Galleries rarely use nonreflective glass, but you must judge for yourself whether it is appropriate for your work of art, and its advantage of no reflection outweighs its disadvantages.

MATS

Mats were not used extensively before the nineteenth century. Today, however, we consider them an integral part of the total frame composition, and we use them to enclose a work of art within its frame. A general rule about the size of mats is that narrow ones should be used with wide frames; wide ones with narrow frames. This is the fashion frame makers have established during the past ten years, and predictions are that it will continue.

A mat has many functions. You can use it either to enclose or to provide a background for the picture. Also, if your work of art is damaged along the outer edges by an indelible stain or a tear, you can "mat out" these flaws, that is, have the mat measured and cut to cover them. When you are thinking of buying a work of art, always consider the area a mat could or should cover. Generally, you will want the signature to be visible, as well as at least

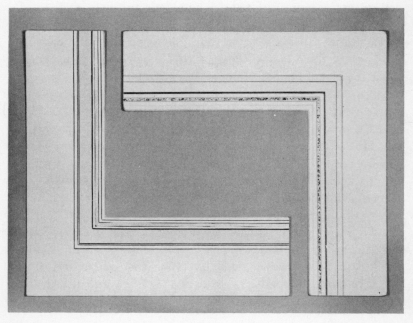

Two examples of French or Empire mat. Courtesy of Dain-Schiff.

one inch around the entire composition. With graphics this method should permit you to see the plate or stone mark.

Mats are available in almost all colors imaginable. They can be either cardboard, silk, linen, or some other fabric, but the most popular and least expensive is cardboard. Museums generally use cream-colored cardboard mats, which are standard and neutral. Regardless of color or fabric, a good mat should have an inner edge that is carefully cut and finished. This edge or bevel forms a frame within the frame. One of the most interesting additional accents for framing a work of art is the colored bevel. A cream-colored mat might, for example, have a narrow, eighth-of-an-inch black bevel to set off the composition within and further define its outer boundary.

A period work of art is often framed with a French, or Empire mat, which has not only beveled edges but also drawn lines surrounding the mat opening. Between these lines there are often washes of color, or gold or silver lines, which serve to further accent and define the mat. Because the lines are usually drawn by hand, French mats can be slightly more expensive than plain cardboard of only one color. They are, however, excellent complements to old master drawings, nineteenth century French prints, English watercolors, and sporting and floral prints.

Occasionally works of art are executed on both sides of a piece of paper, often by artists who cannot afford to waste paper. Some collectors choose to display only the picture they like best. It is possible, however, to exhibit both. You can use a two-sided or double mat, in a frame that is glass on both sides. Such mats and frames have two faces and are usually placed on small stands on coffee tables as conversation pieces.

"Free-floating," introduced within the last decade, is a method of matting according to which an entire picture is placed in front of an uncut mat. This arrangement is ideal if the paper on which the drawing is rendered has decorative edges, or if the content of the composition is such that matting functions more appropriately as the background rather than the container for the picture.

An additional and similar suggestion for matting a work of art, and the most recent device employed by frame makers, includes placing the work between two pieces of glass, enclosing it with a frame, and using the color of your wall as the mat. This novel device, like free-floating, permits you to retain all of the interesting textures, colors, and contours of the papers upon which the works of art are made.

INSERTS

Inserts resemble mats, but are used only with oil paintings. They are linen or fabric areas that are now employed to set off a composition from its enclosing frame, though in the 1880's they were

French Louis XIII frame with linen insert. Courtesy of Dain-Schiff.

used to make contemporary paintings fit frames from earlier periods, generally Louis XIII or Louis XIV, and therefore harmonize otherwise incompatible styles of furniture and painting. Today, linen inserts are often used when a painting has a heavy texture calling for "room to breathe" before the all-encompassing frame is affixed.

CARING FOR YOUR ART TREASURES

Like all delicate objects, works of art require special and careful treatment. A fundamental and all-important rule is to avoid excessive touching and handling of the surface of an art work. When damages occur they are usually difficult if not impossible to fix. Proper framing and hanging is of course the best way to prevent any immediate damage. Nevertheless, even if you cannot always frame your prints, drawings, or oils immediately, you should know the essential good practices of protecting and cleaning them.

As the owner of a fine drawing, pastel, or print, consider yourself its custodian. To yourself, and to those who will later derive pleasure from your art work, you owe all precautions necessary to maintain its optimal condition. The first imperative rule in handling drawings and prints is to treat them with the utmost delicacy. Any pressure from your fingers will leave an indented mark that is virtually impossible to remove. Try to lift them gently from underneath. *Never* use adhesive plastic tapes to mend a torn or damaged print or drawing; after a period of time the chemicals in this tape turn yellow and stain the paper of a print or drawing.

The cleaning of prints and drawings, like their repair, should be left to professionals. Art galleries and even drawing shops or local museums can always refer you to the most reputable restorer in your community. He can steam-clean prints and drawings marked by water stains or other similar spots. His fee is usually reasonable, beginning as low as ten to thirty dollars, and varying with the size, age, and condition of the paper, and with the total amount of work necessary. A restorer can also bleach paper with various chemicals, and apply a fixative to drawings so that charcoal will adhere permanently.

You should never attempt to restore or repair damaged oil paintings; as with prints and drawings, such work is specialized and should be given to qualified experts. But you can clean surface dirt from oils, using a clean, smooth cotton cloth or even a soft toothbrush (which some art dealers prefer), and a mixture of lukewarm water and mild soap. Use straight, short strokes of the cloth or brush, and as little water as possible. Do a small section at a time and clean the cloth or brush repeatedly in clean warm water, continuing the procedure as long as seems necessary. If you are a novice at this cleaning process, remember that it can involve a risk. You might begin with some trial strokes in the corner of the painting and progress slowly toward the middle, always being patient and careful.

To protect unframed drawings and prints you might want to follow museum procedure. Curators use a thin paper hinge and wheat or flour paste to attach an art work to a mat board, and place on top of this another board in which an opening the size of the work has been cut. By using the two mat boards with a margin higher than the face of the drawing or print, you can shield your art work from rubbing or from a similar abrasion. This method not only protects the surface of the art work but also prevents bending and similar mishandling. Moreover, a piece of clear thin plastic between the boards affords further protection. A word of caution, however, about using paper instead; soft tissue paper is popularly used, but sometimes this paper is crudely made, and its impurities can spot and yellow other papers with which it comes into contact. You can best see this occurring in old books where tissue paper is used to separate an etching or engraving from the printed page. Thus, the best procedure is to frame your prints, drawings, and pastels, and to protect them with glass as soon as possible. If, however, you must temporarily mount them, use strong mat boards and transparent plastic-coated paper.

Just as works of art on canvas and on paper are subject to dirt and mishandling, they can also be adversely affected by extreme degrees of humidity and light. Humidity compares the amount of moisture actually in the air with the maximum amount that the atmosphere can hold. When the relative humidity is at 100 per cent, the air contains its maximum amount of moisture. A relative humidity of between 40 and 60 per cent is ideal for your works of art. Be careful and make sure they are not subjected to conditions which might adversely affect them—for instance, a continuously overheated and overdry room or a steamy bathroom where concentrations of moisture are likely to occur. The ultimate effects can be devastating, so try if possible to provide for some measure of controlled air conditioning, which is an ideal safeguard for delicate objects of art and the one now favored by museums.

Natural light can, over a period of time, destroy and dull the surfaces of finished art works. Paintings, drawings, and especially pastels and watercolors should be *kept out* of direct sunlight. In as little time as a few weeks, strongly colored watercolors can become markedly faded and dulled by such exposure.

LIGHTING

In order to reveal the wealth of detail in every work of art, you should take extra care to illuminate properly. A well-designed lighting system is essential for effective and delightful presentations. Lighting fixtures can be attached directly to a picture from behind, so as to fit over the frame, or they can be indirectly focused from a distance to spotlight your special treasures. Lights for attachment to individual pictures are available in a variety of sizes from three dollars up. So, too, are individual spotlights, recent innovations that swivel into position along a single track attached to the ceiling. These spotlights are becoming more and more popular. They are easily adaptable for illuminating both single pictures and multiple arrangements from above or below. Filters that fit over the spotlight are also now very much in favor, as they permit you to control the amount of light shining on your art at any given time of day. Ask your local framer or electrician for more specific information about lighting.

METHODS OF DISPLAYING YOUR ART WORK

Art collectors have devised countless methods of displaying their treasures, but you must always remember that there is no set rule about arranging pictures. Your art work should, of course, be easy to see and "read," since, after all, this is why it is displayed. You can group any number of works in a variety of ways, some of which are more popular than others, but all of which depend on certain basic principles.

Some suggestions on hanging and grouping.

An informal grouping of widely varied works.

Groupings can be in pairs, threes, fours, or more, depending on your wall space. In any case, every picture should have several inches on each side of it, between itself and the surrounding works. Two inches is a generally accepted distance for pictures measuring 8 inches by 10 inches framed, or more. You can, and should, intersperse the various media in your collection. A water-color, etching, oil, and lithograph in a grouping are as well inte-grated as four etchings. You should strive to interrelate not only various media but also different subject matter and periods or schools. If, for example, you are grouping four pictures above a sofa, a seventeenth century engraving next to a contemporary colored lithograph could be combined with a nineteenth century etching and a modern black and white drawing.

A grouping of four pictures of four different sizes and shapes

A more formalized grouping.

poses a greater problem than four of the same or similar sizes. Yet, just as you integrate media, subject matter, and color, so, too, you should integrate frames of various sizes, shapes, and periods. You might place a long, narrow, horizontal, and colorful landscape above two smaller black and white etchings. Similarly, four square works of approximately the same size might be effective if placed one next to the other, all at eye level. Feel free to place gold near silver or wooden frames. It is not improper to display dissimilar frames near each other—in fact, it is more fun, and certainly a challenge to your imagination. Although circular frames are presently not in vogue, it is still in good taste to put horizontal or vertical rectangular arrangements in the same room with antique circular mirrors. This question often arises in the minds of new collectors, but it really should present no problem

Many people intersperse painting or graphics, books, and bric-a-brac.

to you at all.

One of the most challenging assignments for any art collector is the successful wall arrangement of his purchases. Try to make a pleasing composition of the group. Sometimes it is advantageous to sketch your proposed arrangements on a piece of paper. Since you irrevocably determine the site of a picture once you drive a nail into the wall, you should first hang your groupings with gummed hanging hooks, which do not leave a permanent mark and therefore allow for changes in location.

While devising the best method to display your present art collection, you might want to reserve a place for your next acquisition. An avid collector shows his addiction by starting anywhere and hanging selection next to selection at random, leaving the appropriate several inches between each picture, but otherwise being totally spontaneous.

Some people prefer to place their art as focal points or conversation pieces in areas of a room where there is a tendency to congregate. When trying to select the appropriate work for that focal spot over, for instance, the sofa, some collectors often think only in terms of a single large oil painting. You can also consider a multiple arrangement. The focal point can be several works of art, or it can be one. If the final solution is one, then satellite groupings elsewhere in the room are possible, and fun to arrange. You can have one central focal point, or you can have many of them. Whatever the case, you should never feel constricted or limited in your choice of arrangements. And remember that arranging and grouping works of art can extend beyond the living room and library. Today, it is just as applicable in the bedroom, foyer, and office—in any room you choose.

One final point on the arrangements of your pictures—after a period of time, you might try moving and rearranging pictures within a room simply by exchanging one picture for another. You can exchange two or three works of art, or you can rearrange your entire collection, provided that the framed picture covers any faded spots on the wall and that you spackle or repair any nail holes used before. By continually relocating your art treasures, you can transform and enliven the appearance and feeling of any room. Devising methods of display is a challenge and, like all phases of art collecting, it is a perfect and enjoyable pastime.

6   Values, Prices, and Trends

Honoré Daumier, lithograph.

What is this work of art worth? How do I know I'm getting a good buy? How can I arrive at a price for a work of art? These are just a few of the questions typically posed by prospective art buyers—and not always satisfactorily answered. A thorough reply requires knowledge of many interacting factors that combine to determine the final price of a work of art.

Armand Guillaumin, French. *La Ferme* (pastel). Courtesy of M. R. Schweitzer Gallery, New York.

LAW OF SUPPLY AND DEMAND

The well-known law of supply and demand is one of the major determinants of the pricing of fine art. As an artist's work becomes more and more scarce, the profit potential and resulting prices generally tend to rise. The classic example of this phenomenon is, of course, the abrupt increase in price of nineteenth century Impressionist masterpieces, which fifteen years ago were considerably less expensive.

An occurrence related to the law of supply and demand that is unique to the art market is a recurring creation of demand for

Maximilian Luce, French. *Summer Pleasures* (oil on canvas). Courtesy of Sears, Roebuck and Co., The Vincent Price Collection.

artists who were at one time classed somewhat below top rank, but who have gained considerable popularity as the work of their so-judged betters becomes scarce. It has become increasingly more difficult and will soon be virtually impossible to find reasonably-priced works by Renoir, Monet, Pissarro, and the other master French Impressionists. Because of this, collectors today buy the works of Maximilian Luce, Armand Guillaumin, and other less famous Impressionists with as much interest and vigor as they previously sought their more famous contemporaries.

MANY FACTORS DETERMINE PRICE

Although the law of supply and demand plays an important part in the pricing of art, there are other influential determinants. Two of these are the artist's reputation and the estimated appeal of a particular work to the customer. If an artist is new on the art scene, his prices will usually be lower than those of one who is more popular and better established, who has the advantages of a reputation and ready-made market. Likewise, if a work has the indefinable quality that produces immediate and almost universal appeal, the dealer, confident of a sale, boosts the price. But if the subject matter, style, or color of a work is uncommon or bizarre and therefore specialized, he may find himself forced to bring the price down. In addition, such variable factors as the age of a work, changing vogues and styles, the medium, size, condition, subject matter, signature, place of purchase, taxes, and insurance all interact to determine the final price of any picture.

AGE

Collectors often assume that there is a direct relationship between the cost of a work of art and the number of years that have passed since it was executed. They complain, for instance, that the prices of twentieth century art are too high, considering that the artists are contemporary and perhaps living. They think it unfair that Millet's etching of the *La Couseuse,* executed in the first state in 1855, sells for only sixty dollars, whereas an etching by Rouault from the series *Le Miserere,* completed in 1937, costs as much as four or five hundred dollars. But such complainers fail to recognize certain factors affecting the price. The dealer who owns the Millet print probably acquired it at a time when prices were far lower than they are today. Considering the price that the dealer paid for the print a number of years ago, his margin of profit is probably just as high as or comparable to that of the man offering the contemporary Rouault print. There is rarely reason to believe that a low price is a concession to the consumer or that a high price is any higher than what the dealer considers justifiable. In short, there is almost always a good reason behind any price that may at first seem too high or too low. Furthermore, the law of supply and demand is always functioning. If contemporary art is in greater demand than older work, and if the supply of contemporary art is decreasing, the prices will inevitably and logically skyrocket.

CHANGING VOGUES AND STYLE

Similar to other marketable commodities, works of art are governed by changing vogues and by the introduction of preferences for new artists and periods of art. Some artists can be very much in demand during one decade and can then lose favor and popularity in the ensuing years. Other more fortunate masters remain ever popular, mostly because their distinctive styles are what we call classic. Artists and groups of artists can lose favor, even after an initially great acceptance and popularity, and then be revived years later and collected as eagerly and avidly as when they were first introduced.

One of the many unusual aspects of the art market is that its merchandise often has the peculiar capacity to regain lost values. This revival of interest is often caused by books, movies, articles, scholarly study, or museum shows which once again cast a spotlight on and thereby lead to re-evaluation of the *oeuvre* of an artist or group of artists. This resurgence of interest in a particular artist or school causes collectors to seek any and every example of their work, both first- and second-rate. This is exactly what happened in the early 1960's when there was a revival of interest in the nineteenth century Barbizon School. Since then, there has been increased interest and an accompanying price rise in this school of art.

Vogues and the resulting fluctuation in demands for certain kinds of fine art are very often reflected more accurately in auction prices than anywhere else—more accurately, but certainly never exactly. For several years people supposedly "in the know" in the art market have been predicting that the demand for abstract nonobjective art would come to an abrupt end. Yet this work continues to command top prices at auction, and all indications are that these rates will not fall for at least a while longer. The auctions and not the "experts" have, then, the most reliable statistics, for the truth of the matter is that masters like Pollack, Tobey, and Soulages are still very widely and ardently sought.

Just as with abstract art, the craze for Pop art initially saw a rash of harsh criticism from the press, who almost unanimously proclaimed that Pop art would disappear as quickly as it had been introduced. On the contrary, however, it became one of this century's most significant art movements and received great attention at the Venice Biennale of 1964. Many people have been not scornful but appreciative of its re-evaluation and study of everyday objects usually taken for granted. Many have joined Pop artists in thinking that garbage pails, soup cans, and parking lots are significant facts in our everyday life that demand more than cursory examination. And auction prices tell the story. *Gloria,* a canvas by Robert Rauchenberg, was sold at Parke-Bernet Galleries on April 14, 1965 for fifteen thousand dollars. Prices for art currently in vogue usually tend to reach a peak point, then drop off slightly, and finally level off before either decreasing because of new stylistic innovations or staying at a leveling-off line. During the season, for instance, when Op art became popular, Pop art prices did not rise nearly as much as they had the year before, when Pop was the current vogue. Eventually prices of currently favored art decrease, though some of the more fortunate survivors of every school may be re-evaluated in the future, their work again enjoying a flurry of demand.

One immensely popular group of artists is the contemporary School of Paris, whose artists, both firmly established and new, are being eagerly sought and bought. Men like Salvador Dali, Pablo Picasso, Marc Chagall, Georges Braque, Jacques Villon, Joan Miró, Georges Rouault, Fernand Léger, Alberto Giacometti, Antoni Clavé, Max Ernst, Jean Arp, and others are now being joined by a younger school headed by John Friedlander, Camille Hilaire, Lars Bo, Keiko Minami, Bernard Buffet, Kaiko Moti,

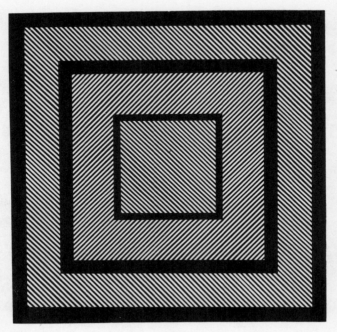

Richard Anuszkiewicz, American. *The Sounding of the Bell* (oil on canvas). Courtesy of Yale University Art Gallery.

Alfred Manessier, and others. The graphic work of all of these artists is definitely within the financial means of the average collector. They are, however, so much in demand that you must be extra discriminating in your selections. Sometimes the quality of popular work takes second place to the quantity needed to satisfy demands, and you may often see outlandishly high auction prices paid for what appear to be inferior works.

Recent auction prices and attendance at auction sales now indicate another new trend in contemporary art collecting. American art is coming back into favor, and auction prices forecast that this vogue will continue for many years to come. After a period of

Albert Bierstadt, American. *Western Landscape* (oil on canvas). Collection of Mr. and Mrs. John D. Rockefeller III, New York.

only moderate activity in the art market, such turn-of-the-century painters as Ernest Lawson, John Henry Twachtman, Robert Henri and his followers are now being re-evaluated and collected with much enthusiasm. Their oil paintings bring a thousand dollars and more at auction, and their drawings are also commanding higher prices than ever before. The auction-price barometer is accurately indicating a new, genuine, and revitalized interest in collecting nineteenth and early twentieth century American art. It is also reflecting a concomitant rejuvenation, a new and special concern for the American art of the West. Our society, though seemingly caught up in the rush of contemporary life, is nevertheless taking time to review the heritage of America as it was cap-

Thomas Moran, American. *Easthampton, Long Island* (oil on canvas). Courtesy of Robert Sloan Gallery, New York.

tured during the last century by such artists as Albert Bierstadt, Edwin Deming, George Inness, Frederic Remington, Edward Henry Potthast, and others.

One instrumental cause of the resurgence of interest in American art has been the sponsorship of Mrs. John F. Kennedy. Through her redecoration of the White House and her care in making the American public aware of what she was doing there, Mrs. Kennedy brought American paintings and other objects of art and furniture to the attention of the whole country. She even instituted a White House Committee on Fine Art, whose sole responsibility was to seek out the most outstanding examples of

George Inness, American. *Near the Village* (oil on canvas). Collection of Lorin A. Boswell, Jr., Fort Worth, Texas.

American art and bring them to the White House. As a partial result of Mrs. Kennedy's efforts, American collectors are now calling loudly for work by artists of their own country. Auction prices are inflated even for small works by major American masters. *The Country Story*, a 16 by 24 inch canvas by Winslow Homer, recently brought $26,000 at auction, an exemplary price for the newly stylish *chefs d'oeuvre* of our country.

Up to this point auction prices have been stressed as reflections of art trends, but they must also be recognized as instrumental in creating these. If an artist's work brings a very high price at an auction, demand rises, and bids can be even higher at the next sale. In other words, once a demand is established at auction, you can most often expect to see further competition and an addi-

William Merritt Chase, American. *Still Life, Copper Pots* (oil on canvas). The Joseph H. Hirshhorn collection, New York.

tional number of dollars bid in future sales, provided that the quality and subject matter of the second work are comparable to the first.

RELATIONSHIP TO OTHER MEDIA

Most artists today work in a number of media, and there is generally some relationship between the prices of their work in one and another of these. If an artist commands high prices for his oils, then his graphics and watercolors will most likely be comparatively expensive. Today, for example, the oil paintings, watercolors, and drawings of Chagall, Picasso, and Dali are currently selling for thousands of dollars each, and, correspondingly, the graphic works of these men also command good prices, from hundreds of dollars to several thousand. At a recent auction at

Parke-Bernet *Le Repas Frugal,* a 1913 etching by Picasso, brought $2,700. Proportional prices—from $25,000 to $100,000—are paid for his oils.

In determining prices of graphics and relating them to costs of other media, you should recall that edition sizes can also cause price variations. Basing his procedure on the law of supply and demand, an art seller will frequently raise the prices of his graphics when an edition is almost sold and the supply is low. The work of most of the masters of the graphic media therefore appreciates after a period of time, so it is best to acquire it when it is first issued.

THE SIZE, TIME OF EXECUTION, AND CONDITION

Though quality should always be more important to an art buyer than quantity, the size of a work of art is nevertheless a price determinant. When buying a picture, your comparative pricing should, therefore, be based on a work of equivalent or similar size. Two drawings of equal aesthetic appeal by the same artist should, for instance, have some relative price equivalence, but if one is markedly larger than another, you can expect a corresponding difference in price.

Still another price determinant depends on just when a work of art was executed during an artist's life. If you are collecting a well-known artist you will probably want to have some idea of his various periods of development and be able to distinguish his early from his later work. Most of the time, values and subsequent prices are highest for the period—whether early or late—in which an artist became established and popular, during which he first adopted a certain distinguishing style or technique. For example, Picasso's early work is bringing fantastically high prices. His *Femme Nue-Assise,* a proto-Cubist nude painted in 1908, was recently sold at Parke-Bernet for one hundred thousand dollars

In addition to considerations of size and of time of execution, you should also give attention to the physical condition of a work of art. If it is less than perfect, the price may be proportionally lower. If the dealer himself has taken measures for its repair or cleaning, the price may be proportionally higher. But if you will have to spend anything to improve the condition of a contemplated purchase, consider this potential expenditure as a direct increase to the dealer's quoted price. A low price is rarely the bargain it appears to be. Repairing damaged works of art can become shockingly costly. Skilled specialists must do this kind of work and their charges vary according to the amount of time and materials they need to make the proper and necessary repairs. Cleaning drawings, oils, and prints can cost from ten to thirty dollars and often more. Tears, stains, and foxing marks (water stains) on paper can be patched or removed, but for a high price. Similarly, oil paintings can be repaired, restored, varnished, and even retouched, but only by well-paid experts.

WHETHER OR NOT A WORK IS FRAMED

While you may have to add repair expenses to the price of a work of art, you *must* add framing charges—unless, of course, your art work is already pleasingly framed. As we explain in Chapter 5, frame prices range widely and are very flexible, but you still should not be surprised if ever you have to pay more for the proper frame than you did for the actual work of art. For example, it is not unusual to buy a print for thirty dollars and spend thirty-five dollars to frame it appropriately. While this is the exception rather than the rule, there is no reason to arbitrarily convince yourself that you must spend less for the frame than for the picture.

SUBJECT MATTER

Artists who are well known for portraying particular subject matter can and do command higher prices for their easily recognizable themes than they do for their exceptions. While it is true that high prices are paid for all Degas originals, those that feature his

Edgar Degas, French. *Gentleman Rider.*
Courtesy of M. R. Schweitzer Gallery, New
York.

favorite subjects—ballet dancers and horses, riders, and specta-
tors at the race track—bring the most money today.

The important legacy of Reginald Marsh (1898-1954) was his
unique portrayals of New York City and its inhabitants from
Harlem to Coney Island. He was and still is very widely collected.
His "floozies" are so famous that they are now synonymous with
any thought of the 1930's in America, and they are the subjects
most highly prized and widely sought after by collectors. Marsh's
wash drawings of boats, while they may be aesthetically pleasing,
do not bring the prices paid for his characteristic subjects of the
Bowery, Coney Island, and the girls of the dance halls. In the

Reginald Marsh, American. *Burlesque* (pen and ink). Courtesy of Yale University Art Gallery, gift of Mrs. Reginald Marsh.

same way, on the contemporary scene, Raphael Soyer's social comments are his forte, and they are accordingly sought after more extensively than any other work he does.

Albert Bierstadt, a master nineteenth century American painter, was one of the most dynamic personalities of the Hudson River group. His sense of light and space gives an aesthetic vitality to his panoramic landscape vistas, and the paintings with these qualities are the ones that bring the current high prices, for minor works by major artists are never as highly priced or as greatly valued as major works by these same major artists. Consider this all-important factor when judging the price of any picture.

WHETHER OR NOT THE ARTIST IS ALIVE

A gallery sponsoring a living artist in its stable usually receives one-third of the selling price of one of his art objects; the artist receives the remaining two-thirds. After the artist's death, his estate usually continues to receive the same percentage, but the selling prices often change markedly. If the artist was successful during his lifetime, they generally tend to rise immediately, and with the passage of time they either level off or continue to increase as scholars and art historians write more about the artist and re-evaluate his work. When Georges Braque died, the prices of his graphic work, oils, and drawings climbed 30 to 50 per cent; all dealers having examples of his work raised their prices. When an artist can no longer produce, the prices in his particular market become subject to the laws of supply and demand, and as the demand increases and the supply decreases, the market rises. But a word of caution is necessary. It is not an automatic rule that an artist's prices go up immediately at his death. This process often takes longer to occur for some artists' work than for others. Sometimes a market will remain steady for a while and then slowly increase, while at other times an artist is quickly forgotten in the wake of a new vogue, and instead of an increase there is a decrease in prices for his work. In still other instances a flurry of price inflations occurs immediately after an artist's death, but weeks afterward the prices level off at a steady, consistent rate to a low plateau. Be careful, then, if ever you buy speculatively right after an artist's death.

WHERE THE PURCHASE IS MADE

The price paid for a given work of art often includes more than the cost of the art work itself, for the dealer cannot help but have other expenses. Like any other businessman, he must allow for the overhead and maintenance costs required to operate his gallery. Since these are added to the final price you pay, you should consider all aspects of a place of purchase in your comparative shopping and buying plans. Larger galleries that do a volume business can sometimes offer savings, whereas the smaller gallery, making fewer sales, must make a margin of profit on only a few items. By the same token, a dealer who pays a considerable sum for rent and for his address probably reflects these expenditures in his pricing structure.

If a dealer is situated in an area where he has little or no competition, you can figure that his prices will be higher than if he were in an area that required him to be competitive. Where there is considerable rivalry, art dealers themselves must "comparison shop" to make sure that they are not pricing themselves out of the selling market.

THE SIGNATURE

One of the most disastrous art-buying misconceptions is that the signed work of art is more valuable than the one unsigned. A person who buys according to this theory might have to turn down some of the world's most highly prized paintings, for many of these were never signed, including the *Mona Lisa* and some of Rembrandt's now priceless masterpieces.

The concept of the signature is a recent innovation for oil paintings, watercolors, pastels, drawings, and now graphics. Yet, despite this fact, owning signed originals has become a status symbol, and an unfortunate one, since it is based on incomplete knowledge or faulty assumptions. Chagall, for example, never individually signed the magnificent colored lithographs of his *Daphne and Chloë* series. Rather, he placed his signature at the front of the book in which the set of forty-two lithographs was bound. These lithographs are presently available to the consumer as individual lithographs. Despite the fact that they are not individually signed, they nevertheless command prices from $350 to $450 each, unframed. Collectors thus recognize that they are purchasing Chagall's artistic creations and not his autograph!

Very often a graphic artist not only signs a work in the plate or stone but also adds his name in pen or pencil to the margins of finished prints. This extra signature often raises the price but never the artistic value of the work in question. Specially pencil signed and numbered examples of a Picasso lithograph can cost as much as five or six times the amount of the same print also issued in a limited number but lacking the signature. For example, *Fleurs* is recorded in Mourlot's recent catalogue (No. 351) of Picasso's recorded works as being issued in 1961. There were one-hundred examples, numbered and signed. They bring as much as $250 each. Mourlot also notes than an additional five-hundred examples were issued but they were not signed. These examples sell for $75 unframed in the market. But price boosts that result from these penciled signatures do not indicate any enhancement of artistic quality. A buyer who pays for a signature may be more interested in prestige or monetary values than aesthetics. You yourself must judge whether you want to buy signatures or whether you are earnestly buying works of art. Do not deprive yourself of some of the really beautiful art works currently for sale merely because they are unsigned. A signature never decreases the value of a work of art, but if the artist sometimes does not think it that important, why should you?

GRAPHICS

The earliest known prices for graphics are those paid during the early sixteenth century for a set of sixteen prints by Dürer from *The Little Passion*. These sold for a sum equivalent today to thirty-one cents. In the present market, however, print prices are definitely on the rise, and have been for several years. This is true not only of the old masters like Dürer and Rembrandt, who have become increasingly more difficult to find, but also of the seventeenth, eighteenth and nineteenth century etchers and engravers like Adriaen van Ostade, Jacques Callot, Robert Nanteuil, and Daubigny, and of the twentieth century American and European printmakers like John Taylor Arms, Raphael Soyer, Adolf Dehn, Georges Rouault, Pablo Picasso, Georges Braque, Marcel Vertes, the German Expressionists Emil Nolde, Karl Schmidt-Rottluff, the Norwegian Edvard Munch, and others. The lithographs of Vertes, which brought forty to fifty dollars ten years ago, now command prices from seventy-five dollars to more than one hundred dollars each, an increase in value of almost 100 per cent. Contemporary black and white and colored graphics now range from thirty or forty dollars to hundreds and even thousands of dollars, depending as usual on such things as the artist's popularity, his aesthetic appeal, the condition of the art object, the demand for specific subject matter, and the size of the edition.

As the size of a graphic edition varies, so does the price of each print; the smaller the edition, the higher the price. This consideration is of course determined to some degree by the artist's production costs, which increase as the size of an edition decreases. Conversely, his costs per unit decrease as the size of his edition increases. A lithograph by the Spanish master Miró in an edition of 150 might cost $200 unframed. Were the edition limited to 50 examples, the same lithograph would probably cost $300 to $350, unframed.

Some collectors deliberately seek the early numbers of an edition, and also try to find examples printed on paper different from that of the first pulled edition. But graphics with low numbers are really no more valuable than the ones with high numbers. As mentioned in the chapter on authentication, a print numbered 49/50 is worth just as much as one marked 1/50, though the impression or coloring may vary in some slight way. This point refers, of course, to contemporary prints only; those of the old masters are not numbered by edition, but often occur in a few states.

People often ask how the prices of old prints are affected by their various states. As described before, states are trials or experiments executed prior to the artist's achieving satisfactory results. Sometimes they are not clear or perfect impressions in which the ink has been evenly distributed, but are instead rather muddy and unclear, some of them undoubtedly unsuccessful attempts in the opinion of the artist. Yet, although two centuries ago collectors were not interested in buying early states, they will today pay high prices for these unique works simply because they are rarities and hence collector's items. Though it is not a very good idea to begin collecting with the absolute intention of seeking rare states, you should decide for yourself in a given instance whether you prefer to own an unusual but perhaps hard to decipher print or a clear and more brilliant but not so rare impression.

EUROPEAN PRICES

In addition to the art-gallery boom in the United States there are also many foreign centers where fine art can be purchased. London, Paris, and Rome are the leading art capitals in Europe. There are literally hundreds of galleries in these cities, some of which you will undoubtedly want to visit if traveling there. However, comparative shopping is a must if you are going to buy in the European market. In many instances, the European prices on name artists or artists in vogue have so skyrocketed that you can very often purchase their work for less money in the American market. This is not to say, however, that all of the current European prices are higher than those in New York. Rather, it is to alert you to the necessity of knowing the existing values and prices in your own market before buying overseas.

The best values in Europe are the works of a particular artist living in the country of the market in question. Once an artist's work must travel from its original source, prices begin to rise. Even in the instances where an artist is permanently represented by dealers in more than one country, his prices can vary from country to country. Montague Dawson, the noted English marine painter and watercolorist, is, for example, best collected in England. His large oils selling for two and three thousand dollars there might cost three or four thousand in America, assuming the existence of an equal demand market. Many young European artists whose work is shown early in their careers in galleries close to home can sometimes be bought there at far better prices than

Nicola Simbari, Italian. *Procida* (oil on canvas). Collection of Mr. and Mrs. Howard Aberg, Arlington, Virginia.

later, after they are introduced into the American market. Here it is not comparative shopping but accurate predictions of future success that can help you determine whether or not a price is fair. Several years ago, the oils of Nicola Simbari, the young Italian artist, were available in Rome for a few hundred dollars; a purchase made then would certainly have been profitable, for his prices are now as expanded as his popularity, being in the thousand dollar range and up. The same is true of Georges Brunon, a young French painter receiving increased acclaim by Paris critics with every exhibition. His unique technique and style have won

Georges Brunon, French. *Silent Reunion* (oil on canvas). Collection of the artist.

him not only a great number of eager collectors but increased prices both here and abroad. He was first introduced to the United States market in an exhibition at the Riverside Museum of New York in the autumn of 1962.

The collector who buys abroad should know that all works of original unframed art can, under the present import laws, pass through the United States customs as *duty free* imports. You must, however, be able to represent them as original. An original lithograph can enter the country duty free, but a photographic reproduction is taxable. For this reason it is advisable for you to retain all invoices or authentication papers for art works you might purchase abroad. (As we said earlier, save *all* receipts and descriptions of your works of art.) If you buy a framed original work, you will probably have to pay tax on the frame, but not on the work itself. So it is wise to have your dealer itemize the prices of the frame and work of art separately.

THE ADD-ONS

There are certain costs which, though necessary concomitants to an art purchase, are tangential and therefore easily overlooked. Such add-ons include packing and shipping, insurance, and taxes.

Properly packing works of art is an essential consideration for their safekeeping and preservation If you buy a picture and must have it shipped, make sure that either you or your dealer carefully selects an experienced and reputable packer. Museums can sometimes suggest reliable concerns, or the yellow pages in your local telephone directory should list a few choices. Packing charges can range from as few as two or three dollars for small individual pieces to hundreds of dollars for larger orders. Inquire in advance about the cost of packing your art object properly for shipment. Though safeguarding your pictures is well worth a sizable investment, an estimate is still a good idea. Don't be surprised if packing charges exceed transportation expenses; materials and labor are always costly. Finally, never estimate packing charges as being in any way proportional to the cost of your art work. All works of art are irreplaceable and must be protected no matter what the cost.

The best and most efficient methods currently used for interstate shipping in the United States are Railway Express and Air Express. When you buy abroad the American Express office can give you the best advice on getting your purchases home. If shipping by railways, ask for the Protective Signature contracts. This is your best guarantee for checking and locating your art treasures if they should be lost in transit. Framed works of art should always be packed for shipping with padding on the four frame corners. Art objects that have glass over them should always be taped with some form of masking tape. Placing tape over the glass prevents shattering in the event of rough handling during shipment. Be careful, however, not to let the tape touch the frame finish, as it may tend to "lift off" the finish—gold, silver, or some other material. Ideally, large pieces of glass should be removed during shipments. The larger the piece of glass, the more the likelihood that it will be damaged in transit. The surfaces of paintings that are not covered with glass are best protected with waxed paper, and if a number of pictures of the same size are being shipped, they can be transported together if they are separated by flat cardboard dividers and packed face to face and back to back. Corrugated cardboard should be wrapped around both framed and unframed objects. Then heavier board should be placed in front and in back of all art objects. This will prevent punctures during shipment.

Whether you are shipping works of art or already have them at home, there are insurance policies available and indispensable for you. Transport companies can inform you of insurance rates for your specific shipping needs. Most major insurance companies now carry fine art policies which cover any or all art objects in the home against fire, damage, and theft—most are one-hundred-dollar-deductible contracts, but they are well worth the money. Investigate your own needs, and if your budget allows for this protection, take full advantage of it.

Other add-on factors to remember when making art purchases are the city and state sales taxes. These vary from state to state and they can sometimes be legally avoided if you can prove that you are shipping a work of art out of the state of purchase by means of a recognized common freight carrier. For example, if a Texas collector buys a $3,000 watercolor at auction at Parke-Bernet in New York, he can save 5 per cent New York City sales tax, or $150, by shipping the work to his home in Texas.

THE CHARITABLE CONTRIBUTION AS A TAX DEDUCTION

Before 1964 the American citizen could deduct up to 20 per cent of his adjusted gross income from his income tax for charitable contributions. Gifts of art works to museums, educational institutions, even the White House, fell within that portion of the tax law. And a convenient provision it was, especially for the clever donor who gave art works to his favorite charity with a proviso that delivery would be made some time in the future, or, as in most cases, on the donor's death.

But all of this maneuvering is a thing of the past, since the opportunity for postponed but deductible deliveries has been eliminated. Yet, still recognizing the need for charitable contributions of art works, tax legislators continue to favor the art collector. Whereas in the past he could deduct only 20 per cent of his adjusted income, he can now deduct an amount equivalent to 30 per cent. But the gift must be delivered before the total deduction may be taken. If the gift exceeds 30 per cent of adjusted gross income, the taxpayer may carry over the excess for a period of five years, whereas under the old law he could do so for only two years.

Although it is easy to determine the exact value of gifts of money, of securities, or the equivalent, every appraisal of a work of art is questionable. You must therefore have carefully determined the worth of any art gift you plan to deduct from your income tax. Auctioneers familiar with day-to-day market prices are recognized as expert appraisers. So are many museum curators, who are also acquainted with market values. And the Art Dealers Association of America, a nonprofit organization, will appraise any art gift, and is highly regarded for its expertise in this field. You must bear in mind that there is no formula, no rule of thumb, no easy way to evaluate the work of art. Only an expert will do, but he must never falsify his valuation. Although the Internal Revenue Service agents are not experts, they do have at their command appraisers able to detect over-valued works of art.

YOU CAN AFFORD FINE ART

Price is naturally one of the most important considerations to both the new and established collector of fine art, but it should not be your first concern. Of greater import is the question of whether you are selecting something you want, something with which you can live comfortably and happily. For this very reason, then, you should hesitate before collecting bargains—that is, before buying fine art just because the price is right. In the long run it is not cheap but expensive to live with a work of art you do not like!

Bearing these points in mind, the collector of moderate means may skeptically ask how he can afford to collect original fine art. The answer is that not all of it is as costly as he might guess. Few realize, for instance, that choice examples of the etchings of Whistler, one of the greatest American masters, are presently available on the market for as little as twenty-five dollars to ninety dollars unframed. The best art is not necessarily the most expensive. Moreover, any family today that can buy a washing machine and other household necessities can afford to own original art, since the same installment credit buying programs are available for both. Consequently, such images as those of young marrieds unable to collect quality art are more myth than fact. Anyone can collect with very little money merely by adjusting his budget to include systematic purchases. Credit buying plans are offered not only by larger galleries within department stores but also by smaller and more specialized dealers.

UPGRADING YOUR COLLECTION

An active and alert collector seeks every possible opportunity to upgrade his collection, to trade or sell one of his works for such a favorable price that he can in turn acquire something of still higher quality, something by a more distinguished artist whose prices previously seemed prohibitive. If, then, you own a work

whose value increases while you have it, you can either sell it at
auction and use the resulting money to purchase a new and better
work, or trade with an art dealer who owns something you would
like to have. Assuming that there is a demand for what you offer,
many dealers and even friends will be willing to trade with you.
Out-of-demand art is, of course, more difficult to negotiate. But
once you have acquired a thorough knowledge of art prices and
values, you will know at a given time how to improve and upgrade your "gallery."

PRICE IS NOT ALWAYS INDICATIVE OF VALUE

The real value of art is not always revealed by the price set upon
it. Something rather inexpensive often takes on a personal value
that no price tag could equal. Value, then, is sometimes but not
always judged by dollars and cents.

Some of the most reasonable purchases in the market today are
works by those artists who were once in favor, lost popularity for
a while, but are again on the upswing. These include, among
many others, the twentieth century English artist Gerald Brockhurst and the nineteenth century French master etchers, Alphonse
Legros, and Louis Legrand, whose work, of superb artistic quality, is now being widely collected for very economical prices.
Many collectors are not dissuaded by the fact that these prices are
not as prestigiously high as those commanded by the men currently working in the School of Paris. Indeed, that price is not
always indicative of value is best explained by the fact that fine
quality examples by Brockhurst, Legros, Legrand, Felix Bracque-
mond, Maxime Lalanne, Jean-Baptiste Corot, and other nineteenth century master etchers can all be purchased at prices below
one hundred dollars.

It is the responsibility of professional art critics to ascertain the
historical and aesthetic values of works of art, but monetary
values you as an art buyer must determine for yourself. Though
you keep a knowledge of value and pricing structures in mind, do

not let the factual information become your only guide and determinant. In the end you will be relying on your own judgment of quality, despite prices, vogues, and other variables. When you have acquired a basic knowledge of the art market, cultivated your own tastes, and developed courage to rely solely on your own judgments, then you have truly become a patron of the arts. Collecting is a learning process that can undoubtedly be one of the most satisfying, enjoyable endeavors of your life.

Bibliography

CHAPTER I.   TASTE, KNOWLEDGE, AND THE COLLECTOR

BELL, CLIVE. *Enjoying Pictures*. New York: Harcourt, 1934.

BELL, DAVID. *The Language of Pictures*. London: Batsford, 1953.

BERENSON, BERNARD. *Essays in Appreciation*. London: Chapman & Hall, 1958.

BRIGGS, MARTIN S. *Men of Taste*. London: Scribner, 1947.

BULLEY, MARGARET H. *Art & Understanding*. London: Batsford, 1937.

CABANNE, PIERRE. *The Great Collectors*. New York: Farrar, Straus, 1961.

CLARK, KENNETH. *Looking at Pictures*. New York: Holt, Rinehart & Winston, 1960.

CONSTABLE, WILLIAM G. *Art Collecting in the U.S.A.* New York: Macmillan, 1964.

DUCASSE, CURT JOHN. *Art, the Critics & You*. New York: Bobbs-Merrill, 1955.

DUVEEN, JAMES HENRY. *Collections and Recollections*. London: Jarrolds, 1935.

———. *Secrets of an Art Dealer*. New York: Dutton, 1938.

FIEDLER, KONRAD. *On Judging Works of Visual Art*. Berkeley: University of California, 1949.

FOCILLON, HENRI. *The Life of Forms in Art*. New York: Wittenborn, 1957.

FRIEDLÄNDER, MAX J. *On Art and Connoisseurship*. Boston: Beacon Press, 1960.

GARDNER, HELEN. *Art Through the Ages*, ed. Sumner McK. Crosby. New York: Harcourt, 1959.

GRIGGS, EDWARD HOWARD. *Art & the Human Spirit.* New York: B. W. Huebsch, 1908.

GUERARD, ALBERT LEON. *Art for Art's Sake.* New York: Schocken Books, 1963.

MABERLY, J. *The Print Collector.* New York: Dodd, Mead, 1881.

McMAHON, AMES P. *The Art of Enjoying Art.* McGraw-Hill, 1938.

PANOFSKY, ERWIN. *Meaning in the Visual Arts.* Garden City: Anchor Books, 1955.

PEARSON, RALPH M. *Experiencing Pictures.* Harcourt, 1932.

READ, HERBERT. "Why the English Have No Taste," *Minotaure Magazine,* VII (1935), 67-8.

SAARINEN, ALINE B. *The Proud Possessors.* New York: Random House, 1958.

SANTAYANA, GEORGE. *The Sense of Beauty.* New York: Dover Publications, 1955.

SPAETH, ELOISE. *American Art Museums and Galleries.* New York: Harper, 1960.

SUTTON, DENYS. *Christie's Since the War, 1945-1958.* (An essay on taste, patronage and collecting.) London: Claridge, Lewis & Jordon Ltd., 1959.

WOLFFLIN, HEINRICH. *Principles of Art History.* New York: Dover Publications, 1950.

CHAPTER 2.   MEDIA AND TECHNIQUES

Graphic Art

ADHÉMAR, JEAN. *Graphic Art of the 18th Century.* New York: McGraw-Hill, 1964.

ARMS, JOHN TAYLOR. *Handbook of Prints and Printmakers.* New York: Macmillan, 1934.

CLEAVER, JAMES. *A History of Graphic Art.* New York: Philosophical Library, 1963.

GETLEIN, FRANK and DOROTHY. *The Bite of the Print.* New York: Potter, 1963.

HAAS, IRVING. *A Treasury of Great Prints.* New York: Barnes, 1956.

HAYTER, S. W. *About Prints.* New York: Oxford University, 1962.

HELLER, JULES. *Printmaking Today*. New York: Holt, Rinehart & Winston, 1958.

IVINS, W. M., JR. *How Prints Look*. Boston: Beacon Press, 1943.

JOACHIM, HAROLD. *Prints, 1400-1800*. Minneapolis: Institute of Arts, 1956.

KARCH, R. RANDOLPH. *Graphic Arts Procedures*. American Technological Society, 1957.

LONGSTREET, STEPHEN. *Treasury of the World's Great Prints*. New York: Simon & Schuster, 1961.

MARINACCIO, ANTHONY. *Exploring the Graphic Arts*. New York: Van Nostrand, 1959.

MONGAN, ELIZABETH and SCHNIEWIND, CARLO. *The First Century of Printmaking*. Chicago: Chicago Art Institute, 1941.

PETERDI, GABOR. *Printmaking, Methods Old and New*. New York: Macmillan, 1959.

PRINT COUNCIL OF AMERICA. *American Prints Today*. New York, 1962.

SACHS, P. J. *Modern Prints and Drawings*. New York: Knopf, 1954.

WEITENKAMPF, FRANK. *How to Appreciate Prints*. New York: Moffat, Yard & Co., 1909.

ZAIDENBERG, ARTHUR. *Prints and How to Make Them*. New York: Harper, 1964.

ZIGROSSER, CARL. *The Book of Fine Prints*. New York: Crown, 1937.

———. *Prints: Thirteen Illustrated Essays on the Art of the Print Selected for the Print Council of America*. New York: Holt, Rinehart & Winston, 1962.

Painting, Gouache, and Drawing

ABELS, ALEXANDER. *Painting, Methods and Materials*. New York: Pitman, 1959.

ARNOLD, EDMUND C. *Ink on Paper*. New York: Harper, 1963.

BAZZI, MARIA. *Artist's Methods & Materials*. New York: Pitman, 1960.

BIRREN, FABER. *History of Color in Painting*. New York: Reinhold, 1965.

BLANCH, ARNOLD. *Methods and Techniques for Gouache Painting*. New York: American Artists Group, 1946.

LAURIE, A. *Painter's Methods and Materials*. New York: Dover Publications, 1964.

————. *Pigments and Mediums of the Old Masters.* London: Macmillan, 1941.

MAYER, RALPH. *Artist's Handbook of Materials and Techniques.* New York: Viking, 1957.

MOREAU-VAUTIER, CHARLES. *The Technique of Painting.* New York: Putnam, 1928.

WATROUS, JAMES. *The Craft of Old-Master Drawings.* Madison: University of Wisconsin, 1957.

Pastel

CSOKA, STEPHEN. *Pastel Painting: Modern Techniques.* New York: Reinhold, 1962.

DAVIS, GLADYS ROCKMORE. *Pastel Painting.* New York: The Studio Publications, 1943.

MACFALL, HALDANE. *The French Pastellists of the Eighteenth Century.* London: Macmillan, 1909.

RICHMOND, LEONARD. *Technique of Pastel Painting.* New York: Pitman, 1963.

Aquatint, Drypoint, Engraving, and Etching

BENSON, FRANK W. *Etchings and Drypoints Volume 5.* Boston: Houghton Mifflin, 1960.

HIND, ARTHUR MAYGER. *A History of Engraving & Etching From the 15th Century to 1914.* London: Constable, 1923.

————. *Early Italian Engraving.* 2 vols. New York: Knoedler, 1938-41.

LUMSDEN, E. S. *Art of Etching.* New York: Dover Publications, 1963.

MORROW, B. F. *The Art of Aquatint.* New York: Putnam, 1935.

PRIDEAUX, S. T. *Aquatint Engraving.* London: Duckworth & Co., 1909.

TREVELYAN, JULIAN. *Etching.* London: Watson, 1964.

Tempera and Watercolor

DEHN, ADOLF ARTHUR. *Water Color Painting.* London: The Studio Publications, 1945.

O'HARA, ELIOT. *Watercolor At Large.* New York: Minton, 1946.

RICHMOND, LEONARD. *The Technique of Watercolor Painting.* London: Pitman, 1925.

SEPESHY, ZOLTAN. *Tempera Painting.* New York: American Studio Books, 1946.

THOMPSON, DANIEL V., JR. *The Practice of Tempera Painting.* New York: Dover Publications, 1962.

Woodcut and Linocut

FICKE, ARTHUR DAVISON. *Chats on Japanese Prints.* Rutland, Vermont: Charles E. Tuttle, 1958.

FLIGHT, CLAUDE. *Lino-Cuts.* London: John Lane, The Bodley Head, 1924.

FURST, H. *The Modern Woodcut.* New York: Dodd, Mead, 1925.

HIND, ARTHUR MAYGER. *History of Woodcut.* 2 vols. Boston: Houghton Mifflin, 1935.

———. *Introduction to the History of Woodcuts.* New York: Dover Publications, 1964.

LANE, RICHARD. *Masters of the Japanese Print.* Garden City, Doubleday, 1962.

VON SEIDLITZ, W. *A History of Japanese Colour Prints.* London: William Heinemann, 1910.

STRANGE, EDWARD F. *Japanese Colour Prints.* London: Wyman and Sons, 1904.

Lithography

BROWN, B. *Lithography.* New York: Carrington, 1923.

DEHN, ADOLF and BARRETT, LAWRENCE. *How to Draw and Print Lithographs.* New York: Tudor, 1950.

HELLER, JULES. *Modern Lithography.* New York: Holt, Rinehart & Winston, 1950.

PENNELL, J. and E. R. *Lithograph & Lithographers.* London: 1898.

RHODES, HENRY J. *The Art of Lithography.* London: Scott, Greenwood & Son, 1924.

SENEFELDER, ALOYS. *The Invention of Lithography.* Translated from the original German by J. W. Muller. New York: The Fuchs & Lang Manufacturing Co., 1911.

WENGENROTH, STOW. *Making A Lithograph.* London: The Studio Ltd., 1936.

CHAPTER 3. AUTHENTICATION

ARNAU, FRANK. *Art of the Faker.* Boston: Little, Brown, 1961.

Art Index. January, 1929 to the present. (A cumulative author and subject index to a selected list of fine art periodicals and museum bulletins. Issued quarterly in December, March and June with three-year accumulations). New York: H. W. Wilson Co.

E. Benezit. (Dictionary of the painters, sculptors, designers and engravers of all times and of all countries by a group of specialist writers and experts), 8 vols. Paris: Librairie Grund, 1960.

GILBERT, DOROTHY B. *American Art Directory,* American Federation of Arts. New York: R. R. Bowker.

———. *Who's Who In American Art,* American Federation of Arts. New York: R. R. Bowker.

Bryan's Dictionary of Painters and Engravers. 5 vols. London: G. Bell & Sons, 1930.

CAHN, JOSHUA BINION. *Artistic Copyright.* New York: Artists Equity Association, 1948.

CUNNINGHAM, ALLAN. *The Lives of the Most Eminent British Painters, Sculptors and Architects.* London: Murray, 1830.

DELTEIL, LOYS. *Le Peintre-Graveur Illustré,* (XIX et XX Siecles). Paris: Chez l'auteur, 1906–1930.

References for:

Jean François Millet, Théodore Rousseau, Jules Dupré, Barthold Jongkind–Volume 1; Charles Meryon–Volume 2; Jean-Auguste-Dominique Ingres, Eugène Delacroix–Volume 3; Anders Zorn–Volume 4; Jean-Baptiste Camille Corot–Volume 5; François Rude, Antoine Louis Barye, Jean-Baptiste Carpeaux, Rene François Auguste Rodin–Volume 6; Paul Huet–Volume 7; Eugène Carriere–Volume 8; Edgar Degas–Volume 9; Henri de Toulouse Lautrec–Volumes 10-11; Gustave Leheutre–Volume 12; Charles François Daubigny–Volume 13; Francisco Goya–Volumes 14-15; Jean François Raffaelli–Volume 16; Camille Pissarro, Alfred Sisley, Pierre-Auguste Renoir–Volume 17; Théodore Gericault–Volume 18; Henri Leys, Henri de Braekelear, James Ensor–Volume 19; Honoré Daumier–Volumes 20-29; Jean Frélaut–Volume 31.

———. *Manuel De L'Amateur D'Estampes Du XVIIIe Siecle.* Paris: Dorbon, 1910.

———. *Manuel De L'Amateur D'Estampes Des XIXe Et XXe Siècles.* 2 Vols., Paris: Dorbon, 1925.

FAGAN, LOUIS ALEXANDER. *Collectors' Marks.* Arranged and edited by Milton Einstein and Max Goldstein. St. Louis: The Laryngoscope Press, 1918.

FIELDING, MANTLE. *Dictionary of American Painters, Sculptors and Engravers.* New York: Struck, 1945.

GEISER, BERNARD. *Picasso, Peintre-Graveur.* (An illustrated catalogue of Picasso's work 1899-1931). Berne, Switzerland: 1933.

GETLEIN, FRANK and DOROTHY. *Georges Rouault's Miserere.* Milwaukee: Bruce, 1963.

HIND, ARTHUR MAYGER. *Catalogue of Prisons and Views by Piranesi.* London: Costwald Gallery, 1922.

———. *Dürer, His Engravings & Woodcuts.* New York: Stokes, 1911.

———. *Francisco Goya.* New York: Stokes, 1911.

———. *Rembrandt's Etchings.* London: Methuen, 1920.

———. *William Hogarth, His Original Engravings and Etchings.* New York: Stokes, 1912.

INSTITUTE OF CRIMINAL LAW AND CRIMINOLOGY. *Aspects of Art Forgery.* The Hague: University of Leiden, 1962.

KENNEDY, EDWARD G. *The Etched Work of Whistler.* New York: The Grolier Club of the City of New York, 1910.

KLIPSTEIN, AUGUST. *The Graphic Work of Käthe Kollwitz.* New York: Galerie St. Etienne, 1955.

KURTH, WILLI. *Albrecht Dürer, Complete Woodcuts.* New York: Crown, 1946.

KURZ, OTTO. *Fakes.* New Haven, Connecticut: Yale University, 1948.

LEHNER, E. *Symbols, Signs, and Signets.* New York: World, 1950.

LUGT, FRITS. *Les Marques De Collections.* (Collectors' Marks). Amsterdam: Vereenigde Drukkerijen, 1921, Supplement 1956.

MANSFIELD, HOWARD. *A Descriptive Catalogue of the Etchings & Drypoints of James Abbott McNeill Whistler.* Chicago: The Caxton Club, 1909.

MAYOR, A. H. *Giovanni Battista Piranesi.* New York: Bittner, 1952.

MENDAX, FRITZ. *Art Fakers & Forgeries*. New York: Philosophical Library, 1956.

MOURLOT, FERNAND. *Braque Lithographe*. Monte Carlo: Sauret, 1963.

———. *Picasso Lithographe*. 4 vols. Monte Carlo: Sauret.

PEARCE, E. HOLROYD. *Copyright for the Artist*. London: Batsford.

RAUSCHENBUSH, H. (ed.), *International Directory of Arts*. Vol. VI. Berlin, Germany: Heinman, 1961.

ROGER-MARX, CLAUDE. *L'Oeuvre Gravé De Vuillard*. Monte Carlo: Sauret.

SAVAGE, GEORGE. *Forgeries, Fakes and Reproductions*. New York: Praeger, 1964.

SCHULLER, SEPP. *Forgers, Dealers, Experts*. New York: Putnam, 1960.

THIEME-BECKER. *Kunstler-Lexikon*. Leipzig: Seemann, 1932.

TIETZE, HANS. *Genuine and False*. London: Max Parrish, 1948.

WHEELER, MONROE. *Introduction to Georges Rouault's Miserere*. New York: Museum of Modern Art, 1952.

ZIGROSSER, CARL. *Kaethe Kollwitz*. New York: Bittner, 1946.

———. *Kaethe Kollwitz*. New York: Braziller, 1951.

CHAPTER 4.   WHERE TO BUY

BAILEY, EMMA. *Sold to the Lady in the Green Hat*. New York: Dodd, Mead, 1962.

BEDFORD, JOHN. *More Looking in Junk Shops*. Chester Springs, Pa.: Dufour, 1962.

BRÉMOND, YVONNE DE D'ARS. *Antique Dealer's Tale*. New York: Putnam, 1962.

BROUGH, JAMES. *Auction*. New York: Bobbs, Merrill, 1963.

HASKELL, FRANCIS. *Patrons & Painters*. New York: Knopf, 1963.

PARTRIDGE, BELLAMY. *Going, Going, Gone*. New York: Dutton, 1958.

POLLACK, BARBARA. *Collectors*. New York: Bobbs Merrill.

RHEIMS, MAURICE. *Art on the Market*. London: Weidenfeld and Nicholson, 1959.

———. *Strange Life of Objects*. New York: Atheneum.

CHAPTER 5.   FRAMING AND HANGING

CLARKE, CARL DAME. *Pictures, Their Preservation and Restoration.* Butler, Maryland: Standard Arts Press, 1959.

FELLER, STOLOW, AND JONES. *On Picture Varnishes and Their Solvents.* Oberlin, Ohio: Inter-museum Conservation Association, 1959.

GETTENS, R. J. "The Bleaching of Stained and Discoloured Pictures on Paper with Sodium Chlorite and Chlorine Dioxide," *Museum,* V (1952), 123-130.

GREATHOUSE and WESSEL. *Deterioration of Materials.* New York: Reinhold, 1954.

HEYDENRYK, HENRY. *Art and History of Frames.* New York: James H. Heineman, 1963.

———. *Right Frame.* New York: James H. Heineman, 1964.

HYDER, MAX. *Picture Framing.* New York: Pitman, 1963.

KECK, CAROLINE K. *How to Take Care of Your Pictures.* New York: Brooklyn Museum, 1954.

KECK, SHELDON. "The Technical Examination of Paintings," *Brooklyn Museum Journal,* (1941), 71-82.

LANDON, EDWARD. *Picture Framing.* New York: Tudor, 1962.

MATUSOW, MARSHALL. *The Art Collector's Almanac.* New York: Treisman, 1965.

MOSS, A. A. *The Application of X-Rays, Gamma Rays, Ultra-Violet and Infra-Red Rays to the Study of Antiquities.* (Handbook for Museum Curators, Part B, Section 4.) London: Museum Association, 1954.

STOUT, GEORGE L. *The Care of Pictures.* New York: Columbia University, 1948.

SUGDEN, ROBERT. *Safeguarding Works of Art: Storage, Packing, Transportation and Insurance.* New York: Metropolitan Museum, 1948.

TAUBES, FREDERIC. *Better Frames For Your Pictures.* New York: Viking, 1960.

———. *Studio Secrets.* New York: Watson-Guptill, 1943.

CHAPTER 6.   VALUES, PRICES, AND TRENDS

American Print Prices Paid; Consolidating the Records of America's Important Print Sales. Boston: Holmans Print Shop, 1947.

AMSTUTZ, WALTER. *Who's Who In Graphic Art*. Zurich: Amstutz and Herdeg Graphic Press, 1962.

Art-Price Annual. London: Art & Technology Press.

Art Prices Current. Sussex, England: The Art Trade Press Ltd.

European Art Price Annual. 9 vols. London: Art & Technology Press, 1949.

FOX, DANIEL M. *Engines of Culture: Philanthropy & Art Museums*. Wisconsin State Historical Society, 1963.

GILBERT, DOROTHY B. (ed.). *Who's Who In American Art*. New York: R. R. Bowker, 1962.

GRAVES, ALGERNON. *Art Sales From Early In the 18th Century to Early In the Twentieth Century*. London: Graves, 1918-21.

LANCOUR, ADLORE HÁROLD. *American Art Auction Catalogues 1785-1942*. New York: The New York Public Library, 1944.

REDFORD, GEORGE. *Art Sales*. 2 vols. London: privately printed, 1888.

REITLINGER, G. *Economics of Taste*. New York: Holt, Rinehart & Winston, 1964.

RUSH, RICHARD H. *Art As An Investment*. Englewood Cliffs, New Jersey: Prentice-Hall, 1961.

SELIGMAN, GERMÁIN. *Merchants of Art 1880-1960: Eighty Years of Professional Collecting*. New York: Appleton-Century-Crofts, 1961.

VAN BRAAM, F. A. *Annual Price List of the Graphic Arts*. Amsterdam: Minerva Publishing Co.

—— (ed.). *World Collectors' Annuary*, 14 Vols. Amsterdam: Minerva Publishing Co., 1946-62.

WARMAN, EDWIN G. *New Print Price Guide*. Uniontown, Pa.: Warman.

Who's Who In Graphic Art. New York: International Publication Service, 1962.

ABOUT THE AUTHOR

JEFFREY H. LORIA was born and brought up in New York City, just around the corner from the Metropolitan Museum of Art, which he visited often from an early age. He bought his first works of art, two Piranesi etchings, when he was sixteen and has been an avid collector ever since. He attended Stuyvesant High School in New York City, and later graduated from Yale University, where he majored in art history. After Yale, he attended Columbia Graduate School of Business.

For several years Mr. Loria has been associated with Vincent Price and The Vincent Price Collection at Sears, Roebuck and Company, in a program of buying original art and arranging exhibits throughout the country. In his work he has the opportunity to know at first hand what other collectors—both new and established—are buying and thinking and the sort of information they need.

Mr. Loria was married in 1965, and his wife is as enthusiastic a collector as he. The Lorias live in New York City. They enjoy travel and the theater as well as the opportunities of visits to galleries and artists which his work and living in an art center afford.

Format by Katharine Sitterly
Set in Linotype Fairfield
Composed by The Haddon Craftsmen, Inc.
Printed by Murray Printing Company
Bound by The Haddon Craftsmen, Inc.
HARPER & ROW, PUBLISHERS, INCORPORATED